A Guide to

Business Communication

A Guide to

Business Communication

WILLIAM C. HIMSTREET
University of Southern California

and

WAYNE M. BATY
Arizona State University

LEARNING SYSTEMS COMPANY

A division of
RICHARD D. IRWIN, INC. Homewood, Illinois 60430

Also available through
IRWIN-DORSEY LIMITED Georgetown, Ontario L7G 4B3

This material published in this book is an adaptation of material previously published in a Programmed Learning Aid (PLAID) entitled *Business Communications*.

Library of Congress Catalog Card No. 81–81552

Printed in the United States of America

1 2 3 4 5 6 7 8 9 0 K 8 7 6 5 4 3 2 1

Introduction

This Guide attempts to provide a concise survey of the topics covered in most textbooks on communication in management. Study after study of the things businesses look for in new employees, and of subjects in which managers and executives wish they had had more training, place communication abilities—in writing, speaking, and listening—consistently at or near the top. These abilities are best developed when learning is followed by practice in a realistic setting. And the modern business environment provides just such a setting. When used for self-study or as part of in-service management training or development programs, the Guide enables readers to apply their learning in actual on-the-job situations.

Although it is necessarily brief, the Guide provides depth in general writing principles, letter-writing applications, and report development and writing style. Chapters on interviewing and listening, oral reporting, and the communication process contribute to the reader's understanding of interpersonal communication processes and of the application of theory to written communication problems.

A person's ability to use grammar properly is essential to effective written communication; and although the Guide pays considerable attention to proper grammar and word usage, the reader should understand that those elements are only the tools for application. Only when they are combined with an understanding of people's needs and of effective planning do they lead to genuine communication skill. Hopefully, this Guide can help the reader develop that skill. The essence of communication is understanding.

A Guide to Business Communication has been written by Drs. William C. Himstreet and Wayne Murlin Baty, both university professors and consultants, who for 25 years have contributed significantly to the literature and teaching of business communication. Their several textbooks are used at the secondary, college and university, and trade and professional levels.

Topical outline of course content

Contents

Chapter 1

COMMUNICATION AS A PROCESS

Business people who hope to be known as good communicators must be versed in several aspects of management and communication. They must, of course, know the field of management, be skillful in human relationships, and be informed about the development of policy and practice in business. Integrate with these an adequate skill in the use of language, and the result should be a potentially successful executive.

THE COMMUNICATION PROCESS

Before becoming an excellent communicator, a person should understand just what goes on when people communicate and should possess a functional, personal definition of the term *communication.* Although information theorists, such as those concerned with computer developments, and human communication scientists from the social sciences work in different fields, both have similar conceptions of the communication process. For our purposes, *process* refers to a particular method of doing something in a number of steps or operations. These steps or operations in the communication process can be illustrated as shown in Figure 1–1.

FIGURE 1–1
The communication process

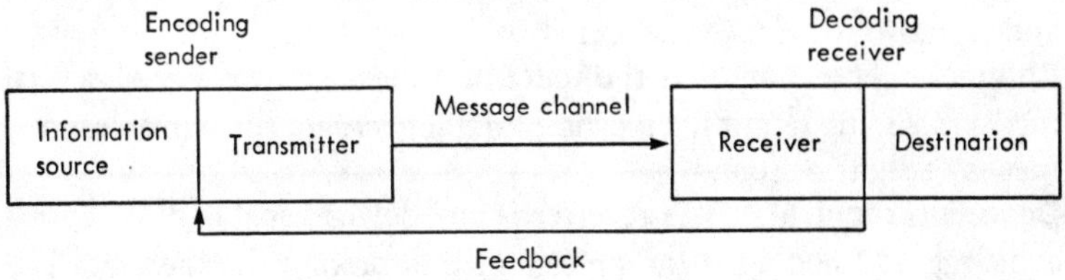

All communication must involve both a sender and a receiver of messages simply because if someone is not available to receive a message, sending doesn't exist. When people communicate—engage in the act of message sending and receiving—the sender *encodes* the message. That is, the sender forms the message from available bits of information. When the message is received, the receiver must *decode*—develop meaning—from the message. This process goes on continuously when we are with others. At this point, let's define some of the terms used in Figure 1–1.

Encoding sender. The message originates with and is transmitted by the sender. Encoding is the process of putting bits of information into transmissible messages.

Information. Information is the property of a signal to convey something unpredictable and meaningful to a receiver. Information can also be described as the "inside interpretation of an outside event." As we experience different things, we develop vocabularies to describe those experiences. Perhaps the simplest example is the way we learn to associate names with people. Through repeated exposures to others, we eventually call people by their names when we see them. The act of seeing another is an outside event and provides the stimulus for our name recall. Observe little children who are in the process of building vocabularies. They have a tendency to point to objects and call them by name. *Train, plane, car, grandma,* and *candy* are examples. As the association between objects or acts and their word labels becomes firm, the information bits are stored in the human mind—the information source—just as the storage in a computer becomes its information source.

Before long, the little child begins to put bits of information into messages, such as "See the train." Thus, encoding occurs and complete messages are developed. The sight of the train served as the external stimulus for encoding and transmitting the message.

Transmitter. In human communication, the transmitter is whatever sensory organ must be used to place the message on the proper channel and to move it from the sender.

Channel. The channel is the route of a message over any of several media including electronic means, postal services, or the human sensory means of sight or sound.

Decoding receiver. The receiver is any device capable of accepting a message. Decoding is the process of interpreting the message. The *destination* of all human communication is the mind of the receiver. The destination is the place where decoding is actually completed. Because the bits of information stored in the receiver may not coincide with the bits of information available to the sender, decoding will always be done in terms of the receiver's needs, attitudes, and past experiences.

Communication is a process that remains incomplete until the message is decoded. The reaction of the receiver to the message is called "feedback." Feedback, then, becomes a message from the receiver to the sender; thus, in two-way communication, participants serve both as senders and receivers simultaneously. What is a message to one party is feedback to the other. This feedback function is the means by which misunderstanding (i.e., faulty decoding) can be corrected. In a sense, communication is feedback.

In the communication process shown in Figure 1–1, disruptions in the message requiring corrective feedback could occur at almost any point. Words, the symbols used in verbal communication, can be barriers to effective communication. If the sender used words such as *amanuensis* and *pusillanimous,* and the receiver did not understand that they meant *secretary* and *cowardly,* the words could not be decoded accurately. Additionally, noise or static can be a barrier in any form of communication. Just as a static interferes with radio communication, unnecessary noise may interfere with person-to-person communication. Information sources and receiving equipment can handle only limited quantities. Thus, senders should attempt to keep message content within the quantity that can be handled by the system. In other words, don't overload the channel.

THE THEORY OF HUMAN COMMUNICATION

The work of Jurgen Ruesch and his coworkers in the field of psychiatry has been foremost in the development of theories of human communication. In addition, behavioral scientists working in the fields of sociology and psychology have strongly influenced the profession of and education for business management by stressing interpersonal and organizational communication problems in the business environment. Basically, theories of human communication emphasize that difficulties in communication lie not so much with what we say or write but with what goes on in our own minds and in the minds of those with whom we are communicating. Bridging the gap between one mind and another primarily by the use of words is the communication task.

The theory of human communication advances the idea of terms such as *social situation, role, status, rules,* and *instructions* playing parts in understanding social action and personal intent.

A *social situation* is established when people enter into the communication process and their behavior is organized around a common task. Within the social situation, each person assumes a *role* based on his or her part in the activity. The role a person plays is mutually agreed to by those engaged in the activity. For example, in the courting process, tradition has established the male in the aggressive role and the female in the submissive role. *Status,* on the other hand, is designated by officially prescribed duties and rights as by organization charts or legal edicts. After marriage, for example, the husband is the legal head of the household. But he may very well relinquish this role to his wife because of the parts they play in the situation.

When status is not readily apparent, such things as job titles, office furnishings, and even clothing serve as symbols—status symbols—to help us determine status. Why does a policeman wear a uniform? To establish status, of course. But more subtle symbols are frequently identifiable to assist in the recognition of true roles. Frequently we find people whose own actions, time with the firm, close relationship with executives, and work habits result in their assumption of higher roles in the activities of the organization than their job titles and other status marks would indicate. Thus the good communicator must be conscious of both role and status and must also use this knowledge in tailor-making messages to the characteristics of the recipient.

All games are played by *rules,* and the game of communications is no exception. Written and unwritten rules, such as company policies and practices, help determine who may talk to whom, how a message should be presented, the duration of a communication session, and what or what not to say. Through living and working in an environment, people gradually learn the rules of the game and must do so if they are to create places for themselves in that environment.

Finally, the area of nonverbal communication is important in human communication. From facial expressions, gestures, and other bodily actions, one can learn considerably more about a spoken message. These nonverbal elements and their implications, along with status and role, serve as secondary messages or *instructions* to assist the reader in understanding the message.

OTHER BEHAVIORAL CONCEPTS

Although all people have some characteristics in common, the composite of our individual characteristics makes us unique. We react in individual ways to common messages. We want to be our own person. With the growing emphasis on behavioral aspects in management, new attention has been focused on understanding humans as dynamic beings with constantly changing needs and desires. As a result, business has adopted policies and practices that are more people oriented than thing oriented. Although it is often difficult to implement, the newer philosophy could perhaps be phrased like this: "The right person for the job" is a temporary solution because people change; rather "the right job for the person" is no doubt a more viable policy.

Douglas McGregor's familiar Theory X and Theory Y description of two styles of management helps clarify the influence of the behavioral sciences on management thinking.

Theory X. The traditional style of management with strong control, concern for the job to the exclusion of concern for the individual; motivation derived primarily from external incentives.

Theory Y. The newer and developing style of management with a balance between control and individual freedom. As the individual matures, the need for external motivation decreases; concern of management is for the individual first and the job second.

In essence, as management moves from Theory X styles to Theory Y styles, external control gives way to self control. Theory Y advances the idea that if you treat adults as adults, permitting them to control their own destinies, they will act as adults and not as children. Such increased concern for the human element will inevitably lead to broad changes in our social and cultural structure.

To supplement the view of MacGregor, we may review briefly the hierarchy of needs concept developed by Abraham H. Maslow as another approach to understanding the changing nature of man's desires. Maslow suggests a sequence of needs through which people successively move as they satisfy their wants and desires:

1. Physiological needs. The needs related to food, shelter, and protection from the elements.
2. Security and safety needs. The needs to be free from physical danger and to be secure in the feeling that physiological needs can be met.
3. Social needs. The needs to be loved, to be accepted, and to belong.
4. Ego needs. The needs such as those to be heard, to be appreciated, to be wanted. These needs deal with status.
5. Self-actualizing needs. The need to achieve one's fullest potential through professional, philanthropic, political, educational, and artistic channels.

As people satisfy needs at the first level, they are then motivated by those at the second level. As second-level needs are satisfied, those at the third level prevail, and so on. Each need level is always with us, however. Lower needs simply diminish in importance as motivators as we satisfy them.

If we accept Maslow's theory about need levels, then we should agree that a business environment which assists the satisfaction of those needs is desirable. In America, most people have fairly well satisfied the lower-level needs and are actively pursuing the satisfaction of social and ego needs. Only a small portion would be at the self-actualization level.

The contributions of communication theorists coupled with the work of Maslow and McGregor, have led to greater understanding of the communication process and of human behavior. Both are critical to the effective planning and conduct of human communication.

HIERARCHY OF COMMUNICATION LEVELS

In addition to the implications for effective communication drawn from the previous discussion in this chapter, we can establish a hierarchy for the effectiveness of communicative situations.

Level one. The most effective communication occurs in a two-way, face-to-face situation where both verbal and nonverbal symbols and languages are apparent to both parties and where instant feedback is possible. Person-to-person conversation is an example.

Level two. The second most effective communication occurs in a two-way but not face-to-face situation. Even though feedback is possible,

as in a telephone conversation, nonverbal symbols are not apparent.
Level three. The least effective level of communication is one-way and usually takes written form in business. At this level, neither feedback nor nonverbal symbols are available.

Although it is important that one do so at all levels, the communicator must do everything possible to prepare third-level messages that will be effective enough to block out disruptions. The good writer and the popular radio commentator are examples of those who have succeeded at the third level. Because this level is the weakest, ample justification can be made to emphasize knowledge and skills in written communication. That is the aim of the following chapters.

SUMMARY

Communication is a complex process, and any schematic presentation of it can only provide surface treatment. Although humans have some common characteristics, they are all different; and therein lies the communication problem. Perception, the process of interpreting sensory information, varies from person to person. We tend to see what we want to see, hear what we want to hear, and oddly enough behave as we think others expect us to behave. Thus, any message may be perceived differently by different people. The good communicator recognizes the value of feedback as a corrective tool. Feedback can be used effectively at both Levels One and Two of the hierarchy of effectiveness. At the third level—one-way communication—immediate feedback is not available. The sender of written messages, then, must use everything in his or her arsenal of knowledge about and skill in human relations, language, and English usage. That is what the remainder of this book is all about.

Chapter 2

CHOOSING APPROPRIATE WORDS

Although words are a primary tool of the communicator, remember that messages can be transmitted *without* words. Such messages are called "nonverbal" communications. They are divided into two categories—kinesic communications and metacommunications.

KINESIC COMMUNICATIONS

Kinesic messages are conveyed through actions. A wink, a frown, a smile, a sigh, a nod—they all convey messages. So do grooming, attire, posture, temper, punctuality, industry, gestures, and so forth. In recent years, the science of kinesics has sought to explain the impact of bodily movements on communication. Some examples of messages transmitted without the use of words are shown in Figure 2–1.

Such messages are being sent and received continually. And they are very important; they determine whether employees can work together harmoniously and whether a business can maintain good relationships with its customers.

Conclusions about businesses and about people are frequently based on kinesic messages. These conclusions determine whether relationships are to continue and be profitable or whether they are to be terminated. Typically, the message transmitted through action will have greater impact than the message transmitted through words. Therefore, business people have to be just as concerned about what they *do* as about what they *say*.

METACOMMUNICATIONS

Almost everyone who has read business letters can recall messages that were picked up "between the lines." These messages are called

FIGURE 2–1

Action	*Possible kinesic message*
A clerk slams down the telephone receiver.	"The message received was not a pleasant one."
A representative arrives promptly for a 10:30 appointment but is forced to wait in the receptionist's room until 10:55.	"The person being called upon is very busy, is experiencing an emergency, or wants to show disrespect."
The president reads a report while a supervisor talks about a predicament.	"The president is not interested, already knows what is being told, or wants to demonstrate lack of concern."
A firm answers all letters within 24 hours after their receipt.	"The firm is efficient and considerate."

"metacommunications." They are not literally expressed in words, but they accompany messages that are expressed in words. Examples are shown in Figure 2–2.

These metacommunications are labeled "possible" metacommunications because not everyone would get the same between-the-line message from the worded message on the left. Metacommunications and kinesic communications have several characteristics that communicators should keep in mind.

1. *They vary in meaning.* To one person, a smile may mean friendship. To another, self-esteem. To one, "Have a nice day" may mean "I like you and want good things for you." To another, the same words could mean "I say the same words to everyone and you are no one special."
2. *They are present in all messages.* All messages, whether written or spoken, convey ideas in addition to the ideas expressed in words. All actions, or even failure to act at all, have meaning.
3. *They may, or may not, be intended.* A woman who says to another "My mother bought a dress like that four years ago" may intend to be stating a fact. Or, she may deliberately intend (with the same words) to transmit the idea "Your dress is for the elderly and also out of style."
4. *They transmit clues about the receiver.* Speakers or writers who appear to make deliberate use of a wide vocabulary may be transmitting information about their educational background or about their desire to impress.
5. *They may make a greater impression than does the worded message.* If a person hears words and sees a clinched fist at the same time, the message of anger and determination revealed through the clinched fist may be much stronger than the message contained in the words. The message conveyed because of a grammatical error may be so emphatic that the idea contained in the words goes unnoticed.
6. *They sometimes contradict the worded message.* "We appreciate your writing to us when things go wrong" may really convey the opposite meaning when nothing is done to correct the problem being discussed. Spoken with a frown, "I'm glad to make the adjustment" may mean "I'm not glad to make the adjustment."
7. *They are influenced by circumstances surrounding the communica-*

FIGURE 2–2

Worded message	*Possible metacommunication*
"I hope you will be prompt."	"Past experience has taught me to doubt your promptness."
"Your complaint has been referred to me."	"Your request has been categorized as unjustified; the problem is so delicate that it must be handled by a person of authority."
"Welcome to our growing list of satisfied customers."	"I want to say something that sounds complimentary but just can't think of anything that hasn't been said already."
"A new generator (to replace the one returned to us) is being shipped this morning."	"The company does guarantee its products."

tion. Today, the smile that accompanies a "hello" may mean warm friendship. Tomorrow, the smile may mean something very different if it follows a bitter discussion in a committee meeting.

8. *They may have either positive or negative effects*. Just as any worded messages can be pleasant or unpleasant, so can unworded messages be pleasant or unpleasant.

No one can give a set of dependable rules on how to interpret metacommunications and kinesic messages. But everyone should be aware of their presence and their influence. Before transmitting a message, senders should check carefully to see whether the words could convey between-the-lines messages that are harmful. If they do, some rewriting may be required. While reading a message, receivers cannot ignore such nonverbal messages; but they should be aware of their presence and use good judgment in interpreting the total message. This awareness of unworded messages and their presence will increase the likelihood that writers will choose the right words for their worded messages.

USE SIMPLE WORDS

Because a communicator's purpose is to be understood, the words chosen should be easy to understand. Long, complicated words should not be used as substitutes for simple words that have the same meanings. When readers encounter a word that is not in their own vocabularies, they may (1) be willing to pass on without knowing the meaning, (2) guess at the meaning and risk misunderstanding, (3) stop and find the word in a dictionary, or (4) wonder whether the word were used for the deliberate purpose of impressing. The metacommunication, "The writer is trying to impress by using sophisticated vocabulary" may get more attention than does the idea conveyed by the words chosen. If it does, the writer has not achieved the purpose of being understood. After picking up the "trying to impress me" message between the lines, a reader could experience a negative feeling that would interfere with the comprehension of subsequent sentences that are written in simple language.

Use of complicated words, then, can result in no meaning, distorted meaning, wasted time, and distraction from the intended message. Therefore, the expressions listed on the left are preferred to those on the right:

about	approximately
done	accomplished
improve	ameliorate
aware	cognizant
show	demonstrate
change	modification
publish	promulgate
chew	masticate

Research shows that "social climbers" have a strong tendency to choose their words from the list on the right. They have a need to impress. Then, one who has the habit of using the complicated word instead of the simple word may be communicating "social climber, social climber" as a between-the-lines message.

However, a writer cannot be expected to use simple words to convey every message. If a word is commonly used in a reader's business, its use is acceptable even though it may not be understood by the general population. For example, one insurance agent talking or writing to another may use the word *actuary.* Its meaning is clear; and, since the word is common in the insurance business, it will not be identified as a word used deliberately to impress. But the same agent talking or writing to a client whose knowledge of insurance is limited may (instead of using *actuary*) use *specialist in determining risks and rates.* Which word (or combination of words) to use is determined by the writer's assessment of the reader's background. The goal is to convey the message clearly, efficiently, and without distraction. Normally, plain and simple words will achieve that goal. One who deliberately uses big words for the purpose of impressing will probably succeed; but the impression may be negative instead of positive.

USE SINCERE WORDS

From between the lines (from metacommunications), readers get messages about writers' sincerity. Even though writers are absolutely sincere, poorly chosen words can convey an impression of insincerity. The chances of getting a message across clearly and promoting good human relations are greatly reduced if the metacommunication is "The writer is a phony" or "The credibility is questionable." Such reactions are a strong possibility when writers use (1) words that suggest certain knowledge of future events, (2) too many adjectives and adverbs, (3) superlatives, (4) words that suggest surprise or shock about others' behavior, and (5) worn expressions.

Words of certainty. Consider such sentences as "I *know* you will want to order today" and "I am *sure* you have considered the cost." Even if the reader does want to order, could the writer really have known beforehand? If the reader does not want to order, the reader is aware of the writer's false statement. "Phony, phony" is the metacommunication. If the writer can be *sure* costs have been considered, saying so may be pointless. If the writer cannot be sure but professes sureness, the statement is false. The reader's awareness of (and negative reaction to) artificiality in one sentence may reduce confidence in sentences that follow.

Adjectives and adverbs. Adjectives and adverbs often add clarity and variety to a message. They are useful, but they should not be overused. And they should not be so strong as to seem like exaggerations. "Our campaign was a fantastic success, primarily because of our marvelously arranged displays" may (because of the words *fantastic* and *marvelously*) seem like an overstatement. "Our campaign was successful, primarily because of our unusual displays" is a less forceful statement, but it is more believable. A less forceful statement that can be believed appears to be more useful to a writer than a strong statement that will be doubted. Overuse of strong adjectives and adverbs in one part of a message can cause readers to doubt the objectivity of remaining parts.

Superlatives. Like adjectives and adverbs, superlatives are useful, but they should be used with caution. Superlatives (words that designate extreme units in series) are seldom objectionable when they are supported or at least supportable. Such expressions as "the *newest* machine," "the *youngest* employee," "the *worst* attendance record" are acceptable when their accuracy can be verified. Unsupported or unsupportable superlatives, however, can cause negative metacommunications about a writer's sincerity. For example, "This is the *best* price you can get anywhere" could be true only if its author has knowledge of all prices everywhere and if the product being discussed is exactly like those with which it is competing. Knowing the small likelihood that these conditions exist, a reader is inclined to doubt the statement. Between the lines, the unsupported or unsupportable superlative says something like "Caution, don't believe it, here's a truth stretcher."

Such a reaction can be avoided if a superlative is accompanied with facts or is sufficiently qualified: "Our price is *lowest* of the stores surveyed: Our store, $141.50; store X, $149.50; store Y, $159.00; and store Z, $169.95." "Our price is the lowest *I know of*" is at least more believable than "Our price is the lowest" because the writer probably has the limited knowledge being professed. Again, a less forceful statement that can be believed is more useful than a strong statement that will be doubted.

Words of surprise. To one who reads such sentences as "We are surprised at your reaction" or "We cannot understand why you hesitate," the metacommunication is likely to be negative. It could be something like "We understand normal behavior, but yours is abnormal and therefore bad" or "We see you as most unreasonable." Having been exposed to that metamessage, a reader may be so distracted that the worded message fails to register as it should.

Words that are worn. Anyone who has read much business correspondence will recall many expressions that are used too frequently; such as, at your earliest convenience, under separate cover, pursuant to your request, and so forth. Such expressions make communication monotonous, and their use is not particularly flattering to a reader. If a boss greets the secretary with "What a neat dress you're wearing," she may be pleased. But if before the day is over she has heard the same statement made in the same words to many others, the words are no longer pleasing. One who uses well-worn expressions runs the risk of conveying metacommunications that say "To me, you are just about like others I know; therefore, I'll use the same words in talking to you" or "You are not really anything special to me." Among the commonly used worn expressions in business:

according to our records
at an early date
at this time
attached please find
permit me to say
take this opportunity
thank you in advance
this letter is for the purpose of
trusting you will
we hope you will
we trust

we would like to
as a matter of fact
we regret to inform

The list could be greatly expanded.

USE WORDS CONCISELY

Since time is so important to both writers and readers, a writer has an obligation to use words economically. If an idea would be obvious without expressing it, it need not be put into words at all. "I endorsed your check and deposited it" would be better expressed as "I deposited your check."

Redundancies (expressions in which one word unnecessarily repeats an idea contained in another word) have long been considered grammatical errors. They also waste time. In each of the following expressions, two words have meanings so similar that one should be omitted: the italicized words indicate correct usage.

basic fundamentals; *fundamentals (basics)**
consensus of opinion; *consensus (opinion)**
each and every; *each (every)**
full and complete; *full (complete)**
true facts; *facts (truth)**
exact same; *same*
exactly identical; *identical*
personal opinion; *opinion*
refer back to; *refer to*
whether or not; *whether*

Additional expressions that employ too many words:

as of this date; *yet, still, or now*
as of this writing; *yet, now*
at the present time; *now*
be kind enough; *please*
due to the fact that; *because*
during the time that; *while*
for the purpose; *to*
in order to; *to*
in reference to; *about*

* Use either one but not both.

in the event that; *if*
subsequent to; *after*
until such time; *when*
with regard to; *about*

Expressions that can be shortened by changing word form:

a machinist who takes great care; *a careful machinist*
in an impatient manner; *impatiently*
work that had not been finished; *unfinished work*
man who did most work; *fastest worker*
man with the most skill; *most skilled man*
tools for which we have no use; *useless tools*
material that can be used; *usable material*
account that could not be collected; *uncollectible account*
person with a lot of energy; *energetic person*
according to the alphabet; *alphabetical*
man of great industry; *industrious person*

The italicized expressions on the right have the advantage of conciseness. But, for reasons of emphasis (discussed later), some of the expressions on the left may at times be preferred. A writer should have the habit of avoiding long, wordy expressions when short ones will serve just as well. But even conciseness can be overdone. The primary purpose of conciseness is to save time. If a writer has to spend an extraordinary amount of time in finding a shorter way to express something, the advantage gained may not be worth the effort.

Compound adjectives can be used sometimes to achieve conciseness. The italicized and underscored expressions illustrate the technique:

The clerk presented some figures that were hard to interpret.
The clerk presented some hard-to-interpret figures.
John gave a report that was first rate.
John gave a first-rate report.
John had an experience that would never be forgotten.
John had a never-to-be-forgotten experience.

Observe that the italicized sentences are shorter than the original sentences. Observe, too, that the compound adjectives (words joined by hyphens and used as one-word modifiers) precede the nouns they describe.

Whether speaking or writing, a communicator has two objectives: (1) to give a clear message and (2) to promote harmony between sender and receiver. If they understand and respect each other, the business relationship can continue, it can be pleasant, and it can be profitable. This clarity and harmony can hardly be achieved without taking unworded messages into account and without selecting the right words for worded messages.

SUMMARY

In selecting the right words, keep the following principles in mind: (1) Rely primarily on simple words; at least, don't use big, unusual words for the purpose of impressing others. (2) Avoid words that suggest certain knowledge of future events when such knowledge is not possessed or impossible to possess. (3) Use adjectives and adverbs sparingly. (4) Use superlatives only when they are supported or at least supportable. (5) Avoid words that suggest surprise or shock about the recipient's behavior. (5) Avoid worn expressions.

Chapter 3

WRITING EFFECTIVE SENTENCES

A writer or speaker chooses the type of sentence that will best serve the twofold purpose of (1) transmitting a clear message and (2) promoting harmonious relationships with the receiver. Sentences may be classified in many different ways.

SIMPLE, COMPLEX, OR COMPOUND

The following simple sentence contains one idea:

> The secretary typed the minutes,
> (subject) (verb) (object)

Because only one idea is included, clarity is easy to achieve. Within the sentence, the idea of who typed the minutes has no other idea with which to compete. Therefore, the thought stands out vividly in the reader's mind. When an idea is especially important, when it deserves emphasis, try placing it in a simple sentence.

The following complex sentence contains a primary idea and a secondary idea:

> (secondary idea) (primary idea)
> According to testimony, the secretary typed the minutes.
> (dependent thought) (independent thought)

Because a reader encounters more than one thought, each thought is less vivid than it would be in a simple sentence. Each shares part of the limelight with the other. But the independent idea (the idea that would make sense if it stood alone in the sentence) is in the stronger light; it gets more attention. When an idea is not particularly important, or when it is negative and should not be stressed, place it in the dependent portion of the sentence. In the sentence used for illustration, the dependent thought happens to be first; but it can come after the independent thought. Or it can be parenthetical, with part of the independent thought coming before and the rest after.

The following compound sentence contains two complete thoughts:

> The secretary typed the minutes, but the committee chairperson wrote the rough draft.

Whereas in the complex sentence one thought has more weight than the other, in a compound sentence the two parts have about equal weight. The relationship of the two parts is indicated by the conjunction that comes between. *But* indicates the second idea is in contrast with the first. *And* would have indicated that the second idea is in addition to the first. Coming between two complete thoughts, *therefore* or *consequently* would suggest that the second resulted from the first. *Nevertheless* would suggest that the second resulted in spite of the first.

When two ideas are of about the same importance (deserve about the same emphasis), this equality can be conveyed through use of a compound sentence. Sometimes a writer must convey a negative idea but (for human relations reasons) does not wish to emphasize it. One way to keep the thought from standing out so vividly in the reader's mind is to place the negative thought in one portion of a compound sentence and a positive thought in the other. For example:

> John has a poor attendance record, but his production record is outstanding.

The negative is counterbalanced by the positive. A complex sentence could further de-emphasize the negative:

> Although John's attendance record is poor, his production record is outstanding.

The production record (appearing in the independent portion) gets more attention than the attendance record (appearing in the dependent portion).

POSITIVE OR NEGATIVE

A "positive" sentence is one that places emphasis on the pleasant instead of the unpleasant, on the good instead of the bad, on what *can* be done instead of what *cannot* be done, on the favorable instead of the unfavorable. A "negative" sentence is the opposite.

Typically, positive sentences have two advantages over negative sentences: positive sentences (1) give more complete information and (2) seem more pleasing, thus promoting business harmony. The following statements in italics give more complete information:

> The job has not been finished.
> *The job will be finished tomorrow.*
>
> The truck is not in its usual parking place.
> *The truck is parked in the president's space.*
>
> The following statements in italics seem more pleasing; they are less likely to annoy:
>
> You failed to give sufficient information.
> *May we have the following information:*
>
> Your machine will not be ready until Thursday of next week.
> *Your machine will be ready on Thursday of next week.*

Remember that, normally, a communicator seeks to achieve both clarity and harmony. Sometimes, however, circumstances require that clarity be given preference. For example, assume a supervisor has observed an operator's improper techniques and says "Let me show you how to get that machine to work perfectly." (The statement would seem more pleasant than "You don't know how to operate the machine.") If that and subsequent efforts result in no improvement, a negative statement might shock the operator into a realization of the need to conform: "You are still making mistakes," or "Improve or get out." But, *normally,* writers should employ positive terminology. Even when an idea is unpleasant, positive words can keep the negative impact from seeming so severe.

INDICATIVE, IMPERATIVE, OR SUBJUNCTIVE

A writer's attitude toward ideas being expressed is referred to as "mood." The indicative mood makes a statement of fact or asks a question. The imperative mood states a request or command. The subjunctive mood mentions conditions that do not necessarily exist. It suggests doubt, supposition, probability, wishfulness, or sorrow.

When writers' positions are such that they can issue commands, harmony between sender and receiver may seem less important than clarity. Nevertheless, commands sometimes sound more brutal or tactless than necessary. If a command is stated in question form, it is usually sufficiently clear; and it may arouse less resentment than would a direct command. "May I have the application before April 10" seems more considerate than "Send the application before April 10." "Will you please turn off the lights" should bring the same results as "Turn off the lights"; but the former seems a little more human relations oriented. (A period—instead of a question mark—is placed after a command stated in question form.)

The subjunctive mood can be employed to keep a negative thought from sounding overly unpleasant. In response to the question "Do you provide installation?" a writer could use "No, we do not." The negative answer could be stated in the subjunctive mood: "We wish we could" or "We would if we had the technicians." The subjunctive sentences go beyond revealing "We do not." They employ positive terms (which sound more pleasant), and they reveal a more considerate attitude. However, in the subjunctive sentences the statement is less direct. When writers are concerned about whether their subjunctive statements are sufficiently clear or about whether harmony is as important as clarity, they should use the indicative mood.

ACTIVE OR PASSIVE

Voice is the word used to indicate whether a sentence subject *acts* or *is acted upon*. If the subject *does* something, the sentence is active; if the subject has something *done to* it, the sentence is passive. See Figure 3–1.

FIGURE 3–1

Active	*Passive*
Bill drove the truck.	The truck was driven. The truck was driven by Bill.
The foreman brought the project to a conclusion.	The project was concluded. The project was brought to a conclusion by the foreman.
The boss will sign the papers.	The papers will be signed. The papers will be signed by the boss.

The passive sentences appear to have three disadvantages: (1) They contain less information (the first sentence in each passive pair does not reveal the doer). (2) If they reveal the doer, they are longer than the corresponding active sentences (compare the second sentence in each passive pair with the active sentence). (3) They are less vivid. When the wording is active, readers can more easily visualize events. They can envision a man at the wheel of a truck, a foreman doing his job, or a boss signing papers. But, in the passive sentences, readers' attention is first directed to the truck, the project, and the papers. Then, after the show is concluded, they may or may not learn the name of the actor. Since passive sentences do not provide a reader with the vivid imagery provided by active sentences, active sentences are normally preferred. But, under certain conditions, passive sentences will do a better job of promoting harmony between sender and receiver.

Recall that one way to achieve harmony is to emphasize positive ideas and de-emphasize negative ideas. In the following sentences, observe that the pleasant ideas are stated in active voice for emphasis; unpleasant ideas are stated in passive voice for de-emphasis.

Active sentences for pleasant thoughts

You completed the job in record time.

John solved the problem.

"The job was completed in record time" and "The problem was solved by John" (passive statements) would be less vivid; they would not provide the emphasis these pleasant ideas deserve.

Passive sentences for unpleasant thoughts

Several errors were made on page 13.

The machine has not been adjusted correctly.

"You made several errors on this page" and "George failed to adjust the machine correctly" (active statements) would be more vivid; they may provide more emphasis than these unpleasant ideas deserve. To the people involved, the passive sentences would seem more tactful.

Sometimes the doer of action is not particularly important. Sometimes a writer may not want to reveal who the doer is. In such instances, passive voice will serve the purpose:

Lunch is now being served. (*Who* serves is not important.)

I was given complete details. (The source is not to be revealed.)

In summary, rely mainly on active voice. It is vivid, it usually reveals more complete information, and it assists in emphasizing the positive.

Use passive voice when the doer is not important or is best concealed. Since it is less vivid, it assists in de-emphasizing the negative. Yet, deviation from these suggestions is certainly justified if doing so best serves a writer's purpose of clarity and harmony.

ABSTRACT OR CONCRETE

Since clarity is so important, writers should seldom employ abstract words as sentence subjects. People and things are easier for readers to visualize than are abstractions. For a moment, try imagining such nouns as feeling, situation, attitude, possibility, or consideration. Since such abstractions are hard to visualize, reading is more difficult when they appear as sentence subjects. Observe that the following original sentences are more difficult to comprehend than are the sentences in italics:

> *Expiration* of the contract is imminent.
> *The contract is about to expire.*
> *Analysis of the situation* indicates that costs can be cut.
> *I concluded costs could be cut.*
> *The figures indicate that costs can be cut.*

Using an abstraction as a sentence subject is not an error; but, especially when vivid writing is essential, abstractions should be used very sparingly.

SPECIFIC OR GENERAL

Just as active voice is normally recommended, so is specific language. Specific sentences give a clearer picture than do general sentences. Observe the difference:

> The president showed some dissatisfaction as he acceded to their desires.
> *The president frowned as he signed the contract.*
> Climatic conditions explain the rate of progress.
> *Heavy snows caused a three-week delay.*

Since the sentences in italics are more specific, they communicate more vividly. But, in some situations, general language may be preferred. When specifics are not necessary, when they are already known to the reader, or when their presentation would provide too much emphasis on a negative idea, general words are preferred:

George received an *acceptable rating.* (When circumstances are such that "acceptable" or "unacceptable" is the only information required, more details would just consume time and space.)

We will be able to make the *needed repairs.* (The general words "needed repairs" are sufficient in this sentence if an itemized list is or has been provided.)

After *your physical condition* improves, please call us. (In place of "your physical condition," such specifics as "your slipped disc is repaired and your leg is removed from traction" would place too much emphasis on a very unpleasant thought.)

Just as active voice emphasizes, so do specific words. Just as passive voice de-emphasizes, so do general words.

UNEQUIVOCAL OR WEASEL

A weasel sentence is one in which its author tries to escape responsibility for the idea being conveyed. For example:

Some would say that the data are valid.
It could be said that the attempt failed.

These weasel expressions convey such metacommunications as "I myself really don't know whether this idea is true," or "I'm willing to report others' thoughts but not willing to reveal my own." Changed to unequivocal statements, the sentences would read like this:

I conclude the data are valid, but others disagree.
The attempt failed, primarily because. . . .

Readers have more confidence in writers who employ unequivocal statements.

SUBJECT-VERB-OBJECT OR EXPLETIVE

The normal order of words in the English language is subject, verb, object. Seldom should a writer deviate from this sequence, as do the following sentences:

There are three reasons for this decision.
It is possible that we misunderstood each other.

In these sentences, a reader is exposed to the verb before learning what the true subject is. Revised, they are more conventional, easier to understand, and a little shorter:

> Three reasons for this decision are. . . .
> The decision was made for three reasons:
> We probably misunderstood each other.

By definition, an expletive is a word that has no meaning. Check the sentence that begins with "There are." What does "there" really mean? To increase the chances of being clear, avoid use of sentences in which a word is meaningless.

SHORT OR LONG

For clear, fast reading, short sentences are normally preferred. For business writing, average sentence length should be between 16 and 22 words. But variety is important. Two-word sentences are acceptable. So are 50-word sentences if they are clear. Best advice for writers: Stay mainly in short-sentence gear.

EMPHASIS

Preceding sections have illustrated various techniques for emphasis of an idea. Now, a suggestion will be given for phrasing a sentence in such a way as to place emphasis on a certain word. (The technique is employed in the two sentences that precede this one. Since the purpose is to contrast emphasis of ideas with emphasis of words, the words *idea* and *word* are critical—they need emphasis because they are being contrasted. Placing each word last in its sentence affords the desired emphasis.)

Since the purpose of the following sentences is to contrast temperatures, the words *hot* and *cold* come at the ends:

> While I was working on the accounting worksheet, the office became too hot. But, by the time I had completed the P and L statement, it was too cold.

Since the purpose of the following sentences is to contrast papers, the words *worksheet* and *balance sheet* come at the ends:

> The office became too hot while I was working on the worksheet. But it was too cold by the time I had completed the balance sheet.

The last word in a sentence is in an emphatic position. So is the first word. A word that should be de-emphasized can be placed somewhere near the middle of a sentence.

PARALLEL CONSTRUCTION

When a sentence contains a series, the units in the series should be expressed in the same way grammatically (construction should be parallel). Notice that the following sentence violates this principle:

> We have three objectives in mind for the coming year: (1) increasing production, (2) to raise wages, and (3) the training of office employees.

The three ideas appear in the same sentence only because they are related. They belong together. Since they are so closely related, they can be stated in a similar manner. The inconsistency in phrasing could cause such metacommunications as "Because they are stated differently, they don't belong together" or "The author is unorganized, careless, or uneducated." Restated, the sentence employs parallel construction:

> We have three objectives in mind for the coming year: (1) increasing production, (2) raising wages, and (3) training office employees.
>
> We have three objectives in mind for the coming year: (1) to increase production, (2) to raise wages, and (3) to train office employees.

People have a tendency toward commonality in the way they dress for certain social occasions. One dressed for a picnic would look out of place at a wedding. When a group of ideas are presented in the same sentence, they likewise should have some commonality in the way they are presented. Otherwise, some will appear to be out of place; and the author will appear to have used poor taste.

DANGLING PARTICIPIAL PHRASES

If a portion of a sentence is not properly attached to the rest of the sentence, it is said to "dangle." If complex sentences are written correctly, the dependent thoughts are attached to the subjects of independent thoughts that come immediately after them. Examine the sentence:

> After wrecking the truck, the superintendent dismissed the driver.

Because *superintendent* comes immediately after the idea of wrecking, a reader assumes that the wrecking is associated with (attached to) the superintendent. Yet, circumstances are such that the driver was the one who wrecked the truck and the superintendent dismissed him for failure to do his job well. This confusing sentence can be corrected in one of the following ways:

> After wrecking the truck, the driver was dismissed by the superintendent. (Since *driver* comes immediately after the *wrecking* idea, a reader correctly associates the two.)
>
> After the driver wrecked the truck, the superintendent dismissed him. (Since *driver* is placed in the dependent portion with the wrecking idea, the wrecking is correctly associated with the driver.)

When a complex sentence begins by talking about action without identifying the doer of it (after wrecking the truck), the doer is presumed to be the noun or pronoun (superintendent) that comes next in the sentence. If the sentence should be so worded that the action is attributed to the wrong person, clarity (the most essential quality of writing) suffers.

SUMMARY

In composing effective sentences, employ the following principles: (1) If an idea is to be emphasized, present it in a simple sentence. (2) If an idea is to be de-emphasized, present it in the dependent clause of a complex sentence. (3) If two related ideas are of about equal significance, present them in a compound sentence. (4) Rely mainly on sentences that are positive; they give more complete information and sound more pleasing. (5) State commands tactfully, perhaps in question form. (6) Consider the subjunctive mood for conveying unpleasant thoughts. (7) Use active voice for presenting ideas vividly. (8) Consider using active voice for presenting pleasant ideas and passive voice for presenting unpleasant ideas. (9) If an idea is to be emphasized, use a concrete noun as the sentence subject. (10) For vivid writing, use specific words. (11) When specifics are not essential, already known, or unpleasant, use general words. (12) Avoid weasel expressions. (13) Form sentences by placing words in subject-verb-object order. (14) To place emphasis on a certain word, either *begin* or *end* the sentence with that word. (15) When a sentence contains a series of items, express all items in the same way grammatically. (16) Make sure the doer of action is clearly identified (avoid dangling participial phrases).

Knowledge of the preceding principles is useful in constructing sentences that are clear and tactful. The art of combining sentences into paragraphs and compositions is discussed in Chapter 4.

Chapter 4

WRITING PARAGRAPHS AND COMPOSITIONS

Chapters 2 and 3 discuss problems encountered in selecting words and putting them together in sentences; Chapter 4 discusses problems encountered in combining sentences into paragraphs and making the paragraphs into complete compositions.

PARAGRAPHS

When paragraphing is done carelessly, readers may have difficulty in understanding the material and also may draw uncomplimentary conclusions about the author's ability to organize and express himself clearly.

Imagine the difficulty in reading a long composition that is not divided into paragraphs. The pages would all look the same. Until getting into the next sentence a reader would not know whether it is about a new topic or just further discussion of a preceding topic, and major ideas would not stand out any more vividly than minor ideas.

The typical letter, report, or speech contains a limited number of major ideas. Each major idea requires supporting details. The typical paragraph has one sentence that conveys the major idea and enough additional sentences to complete the discussion of that idea.

The major idea can be first in the paragraph, or it can be last. Either position is acceptable. Naturally, the major idea deserves more emphasis than do the supporting details. Just as the first and last words in a sentence are in emphatic positions, so are the first and last sentences in a paragraph.

When the major idea appears in the first sentence of a paragraph, a reader gets a preliminary idea of what to expect in remaining sentences—support for the point just made. Since this arrangement has the effect of letting a reader know what to expect, the reading is fast and easy. To review the major points, a reader has but to re-read first sentences of paragraphs.

When the major idea appears in the last sentence of a paragraph, it is not likely to come as a surprise. As a result of exposure to the details that precede, a reader may see the major idea as logical. It may come as confirmation of a generalization of details already generated in the reader's mind. To review major points, a reader has but to re-read last sentences of paragraphs.

A writer should choose the pattern that best serves the purpose of the message. The deductive arrangement (major sentence first) has the advantage of quickly revealing the subject of the paragraph and making reading easy. The inductive arrangement (major sentence last) is more useful when persuasion is necessary or when (without preliminary justification) major ideas might be rejected. For example, assume upon reading the first sentence of a paragraph that the reader's reaction is "I disagree," "The author is illogical," or "I don't see why." From that point on, the reader may (instead of trying to understand the supporting details) try harder to seek rebuttal, to find support for the initial negative reaction. If the same major idea had been written *after* the details, a negative reaction could have been avoided. Clarity and writer-reader harmony might have been achieved.

The major idea in a paragraph can be in some position other than first or last. If for some reason a writer wants to precede (and then follow) a major thought with detail, the technique is justified. Two suggestions, however: (1) First and last positions afford the emphasis a major idea deserves. (2) Readers appreciate consistency on the part of writers. After a few paragraphs, a reader becomes familiar with the writer's pattern and feels more comfortable if it is followed fairly consistently.

Paragraph length is determined by the amount of detail necessary to complete the discussion of a general idea. The more involved an idea, the more supporting detail required and the longer the paragraph. Some paragraphs, then, will be much shorter than others. This variety in length is natural and welcomed. If supporting details are not necessary, one-sentence paragraphs are acceptable. Among longer paragraphs, a one-sentence paragraph stands out vividly.

Compared with short paragraphs, long paragraphs look less inviting to read. For a reader, the end of a paragraph is a resting point—a stopping place for some clinching or reflecting upon the points just made. If the upcoming paragraph is extraordinarily long, the reading task may look formidable.

In business reports, paragraphs are usually longer than in business letters. Reports are about more complicated subjects and require more details. In report paragraphs, an idea that requires more than eight or ten lines of support can be profitably broken into two separate ideas each of which can be supported in fewer lines. In letters, a paragraph is on the verge of being too long if it has more than five or six lines. To give first and last sentences the emphasis they deserve, and to make letters look inviting to read, first and last paragraphs are kept short—from one to no more than three or four lines.

Within paragraphs, the sentences should lead a reader naturally from one to the next. If they do not, the reader may be lost or clarity may be reduced. To avoid these possibilities, writers need to be especially careful in applying their techniques of coherence.

Coherence (the quality of cohesiveness in which one sentence leads naturally into the next) is fairly easy to achieve when the writing is narrative. Just telling next what happened next is not difficult. But coherence is more difficult to achieve when the writing is expository (presents and explains ideas). Since business letters and reports are expository, one who writes them needs to have a good command of various coherence techniques.

Lincoln employed those techniques masterfully in the Gettsburg Address. (See Figure 4–1.) The same technique he used can be applied in business writing. Observe how the underlined words (not underlined in the original, of course) serve to tie each sentence to the next. Read each numbered sentence on the left, and then read the commentary on the right.

Although the Address is known primarily for its noble thoughts, it is a masterpiece of coherence. Business writers can employ the same techniques Lincoln used:

1. Have good ideas and arrange them in logical order.
2. Repeat nouns introduced in previous sentences.
3. Use a pronoun in one sentence to stand for a noun introduced in an earlier sentence.
4. Give a word signal when the topic is about to change.

Such joining words as *and, but, for, because, therefore, however, thus,* and *consequently,* are especially useful in leading the reader natu-

FIGURE 4–1

(1) Fourscore and seven years ago our fathers brought forth on this continent a new nation, conceived in liberty, and dedicated to the proposition that all men are created equal.	
(2) Now we are engaged in a great civil war, testing whether that nation, or any nation so conceived and so dedicated, can long endure.	(2) Grows naturally out of sentence (1). "That nation" can only refer to the "new nation" of the previous sentence. "So conceived" and "so dedicated" are emphatic repetitions of words introduced in the first sentence.
(3) We are met on a great battlefield of that war.	(3) "That war" refers to the "great civil war" mentioned in sentence (2).
(4) We have come to dedicate a portion of that field as a final resting-place for those who here gave their lives that that nation might live.	(4) "That field" refers to the "great battlefield" in sentence (3). "That nation" refers to the "new nation" spoken of in the first sentence.
(5) It is altogether fitting and proper that we should do this.	(5) "This" refers to "dedicate a portion" in sentence (4).
(6) But, in a larger sense, we cannot dedicate—we can not consecrate—we cannot hallow . . .	(6) The "but" beginning ties this sentence to preceding sentences; at the same time, it suggests we have approached a turn in the discourse. For now "we cannot" do the dedicating mentioned earlier.

rally from one sentence to the next sentence and from one paragraph to the next paragraph.

COMPOSITIONS

Preceding discussions have been limited to smaller units of a composition—words, sentences, and paragraphs. But high standards in these elements alone do not assure successful writing of an entire composition. Before, during, and after the composition of sentences and paragraphs, a writer needs to keep some broader problems in mind: the thesis statement, unity, emphasis, sequence, readability, grammar, and mechanics.

The thesis statement. In the typical letter, report, or speech, the communicator has a central idea to convey. Whether it is called "thesis," "theme," or "central idea," it is the one broad thought that is to be transmitted. All sentences and paragraphs contribute to that thought. When writers find themselves composing sentences that do not contribute to the primary thought, the sentences should be cut.

One of the best ways to reduce the probability of getting off the main subject is to *write down a statement of the thesis before beginning the composition.* In a letter, the thesis statement may be "For good reason, your request must be denied." In a report, it may be "A formal merit-rating system should be instituted." In a prepared speech, it may be "Let's revise our marketing strategy." By putting such thesis statements *on paper* before beginning to write, one who prepares a message decreases the likelihood of straying from the main topic.

Unity. The main topic, the general idea of a message, should be evident from the beginning. All sentences should be related to it. The finished message should seem like a completed unit. In a report or speech, unity is achieved by introducing the central idea, presenting the related details, and returning to the central idea in the closing sentences. In a letter, unity is achieved by making sure the first sentence sounds like an appropriate beginning and that the last sentence sounds like an appropriate ending. If the last sentence is in some way related to the first, the unit will seem to have been completed. Otherwise, the closing will seem abrupt—as if the writer just quit before reaching the end.

Emphasis. The closing sentence of a composition is in an emphatic position. So is the beginning sentence. In reports, nothing deserves more emphasis than does the thesis. Placing it at the beginning and at the end provides emphasis as well as unity. Another way to emphasize the thesis is by making repeated references to it. Those references are necessary and expected. By definition, a thesis is an idea that permeats an entire message.

To emphasize a certain point in a message, a writer can (1) devote considerably more space to it than to other points; (2) put it in first or last position among other points; (3) label it as being more significant than other points; (4) underscore it or type in capital letters; or (5) employ emphasis techniques that appear in preceding discussions of words, sentences, and paragraphs.

Sequence. As pointed out in preceding pages, writers can achieve their purposes by placing a word in its proper position within a sentence and by placing a sentence in its proper position within a paragraph. Likewise, paragraphs need to be arranged in the most appropriate sequence within the entire composition. In letters, the sequence can be readily determined by anticipating the probable reader reaction (see next chapter). In reports, a writer may select from the following sequences:

Space order moves from that which is near to that which is far. A report about branch offices could begin with the office nearest and end with the office farthest from the main office.

Chronological order relates a sequence of events in the order in which they happened. A discussion on legislative enactments could begin with the first one passed and end with the last one.

Familiar-to-unfamiliar order begins with those points about which readers may know most and proceeds to those about which they know least. A set of instructions on how to operate a new machine could begin by first reviewing the operation of a machine with which the reader is familiar, and then proceed to point out basic similarities of the steps in operating the unfamiliar one.

Deductive and inductive order applies to the sequence of paragraphs as well as to the sequence of sentences within paragraphs. A major conclusion could be presented in one paragraph and supported in subsequent paragraphs (deductive sequence), the supporting paragraphs could be presented first (inductive sequence).

Closeness in relationship justifies putting ideas close together. Since cost of upkeep is related to initial cost, and since durability and upkeep are related, the sequence of paragraphs could be initial cost, cost of upkeep, and durability.

Order of importance begins with the most important ideas and ends with the least important ones, or begins with the least important ideas and ends with the most important ones. The arrangement assists in placing emphasis where it is most desired.

If the sequence of paragraphs and major units of a composition have been well planned, the next topic to be taken up will seem to the reader as a logical next topic. To bridge the gap that sometimes seems to occur between major units of a composition, good writers employ transition sentences. In addition to providing a summary of the major unit from which the writer is emerging, transition sentences subtly lead the reader to expect the next major unit. They confirm the logic of the sequence and add to coherence within the whole composition.

Whatever the arrangement of paragraphs, it should be decided upon before the composition is begun. If not, the writer will have a sense of insecurity as the writing progresses; the reader will have a difficult chore.

Readability. In preceding pages, short sentences and simple words have been recommended. If they are employed, fast reading and clear understanding are possible. Formulas for checking the reading-difficulty level are presented in Robert Gunning's *The Technique of Clear Writing* (McGraw-Hill, 1952) and Rudolph Flesch's *The Art of Readable Writing* (Harper and Row, 1949). Normally, a suitable level for business people is somewhere between the 8th and the 11th grade levels. Even though they may have a college or graduate-level education, they appreciate a message that is quickly and easily understood.

Although writers have been encouraged to rely primarily on simple words, a good vocabulary is still useful. It not only improves the chances of finding just the right word when writing, it also improves the chances of understanding when reading.

Grammar. Since writing is a complicated activity, success is more likely if it is undertaken a part at a time. First, decide what to say and the sequence. Second, say it (not deliberately neglecting grammar, but concentrating primarily on getting the message on paper). Third, proofread and correct grammatical errors before the final draft is typed. Errors in grammar can cause (1) misunderstanding, (2) loss of time,

(3) distraction from the ideas presented, and (4) negative metacommunications about the writer.

Mechanics. Before releasing a letter or the final draft of a report, a writer should likewise check carefully for errors in spelling, punctuation, and typing. The consequences of mechanical errors are about the same as the consequences of grammatical errors. They interfere with clarity and harmony—the twin goals of a writer.

SUMMARY

The typical paragraph contains a major idea and a limited number of supporting ideas. Although the major idea is sometimes preceded and followed by supporting ideas, the typical paragraph either begins or ends with the major idea. Deductive paragraphs begin with the major idea; inductive paragraphs end with the major ideas. Unless a writer has some reason for changing, consistency is recommended. When a message is persuasive, inductive paragraphs are recommended.

Because the amount of support for major ideas varies, paragraphs cannot be expected to have uniform length. In reports, paragraphs seldom should be more than 8 or 10 lines long; in letters, a paragraph of more than five or six lines is approaching maximum length.

If paragraphs are coherent, one sentence leads naturally to the next; abrupt changes in thought will not occur. Some specific coherence techniques: (1) Arrange ideas in logical order. (2) Repeat nouns introduced in preceding sentences. (3) Use pronouns with antecedents in preceding sentences. (4) Use connecting words (such as *and, but,* and *therefore*) when the topic is about to change.

Just as sentences form a paragraph, paragraphs form a composition. Some important considerations for building paragraphs into an entire composition: (1) Before composing, write down the thesis statement; include only sentences and paragraphs that contribute to its support. (2) Develop unity by introducing the central idea at the beginning, following with related details, and restating the central idea in closing sentences. (3) Emphasize the central idea by making frequent references to it; for other points that deserve emphasis, devote more space, label as being significant, underscore or type in capital letters, or employ other emphasis techniques that appear in preceding discussions of sentences and paragraphs. (4) Before composing, choose the most desirable sequence of paragraphs (space order, chronological order, familiar-to-unfamiliar order, deductive or inductive order, closeness in relationship, or order of importance). (5) Relying mainly on short sentences and commonly used words, strive normally for a readability level between grades 8 and 11. (6) Strive for perfection in grammar and mechanics; if errors occur, the result is misunderstanding, loss of time, distraction from the ideas being conveyed, and a negative impression of the writer.

Chapter 5

PLANNING MESSAGES FOR READER REACTION

Preceding chapters illustrate the complexity of communication. In one short letter, the author has many decisions to make about words, sentences, and paragraphs. The task is even more complicated if (while making these decisions) the writer is also concerned about whether the message is what it really should be, or whether thoughts are being presented in the right sequence. To simplify the process, to make the end result more effective, and to save time, a communicator should plan the entire message carefully before beginning to write the letter.

Just as a traveler makes plans before departing, just as a builder makes blueprints before beginning construction, so should a writer get answers to certain questions before putting the first sentence on paper:

1. Is the letter designed to convey the *right message?* If the letter is intended to convey a decision, the writer should be convinced that it is a fair decision. In the absence of that conviction, doubts may complicate the writing and negative metacommunications may creep into the reading. If the letter is intended to make a request, the writer should be convinced that it is legitimate. Otherwise, the writing task should not be undertaken. If a letter is written impulsively, it may not really convey the right message. Although procrastination should not be allowed to become a habit, one who impulsively decides to

send an emotionally charged letter should probably wait a day or two—just to see if the thoughts are still appropriate.

2. Is the letter being written for the *right purpose?* The purpose should be to communicate an idea clearly and to promote harmonious relationships with the reader. If a letter is being prepared for any other purpose (to impress, to flatter, to humiliate) its value is questionable.

3. Is the letter likely to evoke *an emotional reaction?* Answering this question helps the writer to employ empathy—to project into the viewpoint of the receiver. It also forces the writer to consider the reader's background and attitudes. Such preliminary thinking increases the probability that the letter will be tactful.

4. Should the sequence be *inductive or deductive?* Reader reaction (preceding question) determines the answer to this question. Readers react in one of four ways: *pleased* about the message, *interested* in the message but not emotionally involved, *displeased* about the message, or *not interested* initially and will have to be persuaded.

Although no two individuals are alike, people do have commonality in their behavior. To predict a reader's reaction to a message that is being planned, a writer has but to ask "What would my own reaction be?" The answer determines whether the letter should be written inductively or deductively.

DEDUCTIVE LETTERS

Recall that the deductive arrangement presents the main idea first and follows with details. When the reader will be pleased, or when the reader will be interested but not emotionally involved, the deductive arrangement is preferred.

When the reader will be pleased. Writers can be fairly certain that readers will be pleased to learn that a refund is being made, an order is being shipped on schedule, credit is being granted, or an invitation is being accepted. Confident that the message is based on a fair decision and that the reader's reaction is going to be favorable, a writer is not quite ready to begin composing the first sentence. Composition of the entire letter will be simplified if a brief outline is made first. Having first made the decisions about what the ideas should be and the order in which to present them, a writer can (while composing) concentrate totally on how to express them. Presenting good news is easy, and the writing is easy when the following outline is applied:

1. In the first sentence, present the most pleasant aspect of the communication.
2. Follow with details or explanations.
3. Close with a sentence that either reminds the recipient of the pleasant thought or looks positively to the future.

The following letter illustrates application of this deductive sequence. Italicized words are inserted to illustrate application of the preceding outline.

> Yes, you are entitled to a $100 refund (check enclosed).
>
> *Begins with the pleasant thought.*
>
> When your March statement was sent, your purchase return of March 10 had not been recorded. We appreciate your full and prompt payment of the invoice and your letting us know about the possibility of an overcharge to your account.
>
> *Adds explanations (details).*
>
> With the new equipment recently installed, we can process your next order on the date received.
>
> *Alludes confidently to future transactions.*

The pleasant-thought-first pattern in the preceding letter has the following advantages:

1. It emphasizes the pleasant idea by placing it in the first sentence—where it will stand out vividly in the reader's mind.
2. It immediately puts readers in a positive frame of mind, prepares them for quick and easy understanding of details that follow.
3. It provides writers with a dependable aid in getting a letter started. They waste no time in wondering how to begin. Now that the primary idea is on paper, the rest follows easily.

The pattern for writing letters in which the reader will be interested but not emotionally involved is similar.

When the reader will be interested but not emotionally involved. Much of the correspondence that passes in business contains routine information—that is wanted or expected but which can be neither classified as good news nor bad news. Like other letters, they contain a primary idea and support or explanations. The following outline is recommended:

1. Put the primary idea in the first sentence.
2. Follow with details or explanations.
3. Choose an appropriate closing. The closing sentence can refer to the main idea, identify action the reader is to take, or express appreciation.

The following letter illustrates application of these points. Since it is a request for information, it is not expected to be received as good news or bad news; but the reader (who is in the business of selling machines) should be interested.

> Please send me information about the cost, speed, and space requirements of your machine accounting equipment.
>
> *Reveals the primary purpose of the letter.*
>
> I am especially interested in buying equipment that could do the following tasks: (1) Initial entry and posting of about 4,000 invoices a month. (2) Payroll accounting for 300 employees paid weekly. (3) Perpetual inventory records for about 150 items.
>
> *Follows with explanatory details.*
>
> Because our present accounting staff is unable to keep up with the current volume by doing the work manually, I shall appreciate your quick answers to these question.
>
> *Refers to main idea and action desired.*

The primary-idea-first pattern in the preceding letter has the following advantages:

1. It saves time for the recipient. The clerks opening the mail can readily identify the desk to which the letter should be sent for reply. The reader can determine quickly what the whole letter is about.
2. It emphasizes the primary idea by placing it at the beginning.
3. It simplifies composition. Once the important idea is stated, remaining sentences fall naturally into place.

INDUCTIVE LETTERS

When the reader will be displeased or will have to be persuaded, the inductive arrangement is preferred.

When the reader will be displeased. Compared with the task of conveying good news, the task of conveying bad news is more challenging. Seldom can writers convey bad news in such a way as to make readers happier than they would have been with good news. That much success is not expected. But because relationships may be strained as a result of what the message *is*, writers should be especially careful about *how it is conveyed.* If the message itself is justified, and if it is presented with tact, the cordial reader–writer relationship may be preserved.

If the message (bad news) is justified, the writer will have solid reasons to support the decision. If the reasons are read and understood, the decision may be accepted without resentment. The reasons, then, become the key to harmonious relationships. The reasons deserve emphasis, more emphasis than they would get if the negative decision were presented first.

Suppose, for example, that a refusal letter begins with the following statement:

> Your request for reimbursement has been denied.

A reader who had previously submitted what was thought to be a legitimate request would almost certainly disagree. In that mental state, the reader's receptivity to explanations would be reduced. If the reaction to the first sentence is "I didn't get fair treatment," "The decision was arbitrary," or other negative reactions, the explanations may not be read at all. Or instead of keeping an open mind and trying to understand the explanations, the reader may instead concentrate on rebuttal as each remaining sentence is read. And, having reacted with "This is unjust" upon reading the first sentence, a reader could (because of a sensitive ego) refuse to modify the reaction even though the reasons are very solid. These obstacles can be partially overcome by presenting *reasons before* presenting a major thought that is negative. The following outline is recommended:

1. Begin with a pleasant or neutral statement—one that neither identifies the news as good nor bad but leads to a discussion of reasons.

2. Present the facts, give the supporting reasons.
3. State the negative idea.
4. Close with a positive or neutral statement.

While shopping at a department store, a customer stopped at the office, asked the amount of her indebtedness, and wrote a check for the amount quoted. After receiving a statement for $27, the customer wrote a letter asking that the $27 charge be dropped. The following letter employs inductive sequence; it was designed to let the customer know that the charge was not to be written off.

A look at your card revealed the answer to the question raised in your letter of October 27.

Neutral statement, reveals what the letter is about, leads to a presentation of explanations.

	Purchases	*Payments*	*Balance*
September 21	20.00		20.00
October 1	44.17		64.17
October 8	10.56		74.73
October 19		47.73	27.00

The clerk who reported your balance obviously read the dollar digits in reverse order (47 instead of 74). If she had overstated your balance and you had paid the amount quoted, you would have had a credit toward future purchases.

Provides reasons for the refusal.

Since the amount was understated, your account shows the $27 balance. Since it is for purchases made, it is your obligation; but, if payment is received before November 15, the amount is interest free.

Reveals that the customer is not being excused from paying.

The clerk recognizes the consequences of the transposition, is genuinely sorry about it, and will keep trying to achieve perfection in handling figures.

Thank you for making your latest payment before receiving a bill.

Closes with a positive statement.

The inductive pattern in the preceding letter has the following advantages:

1. The first sentence reveals that the letter is *about* a problem (the apparent overcharge) without stating the *negative answer* to it (you

can't be excused from paying). Because the first sentence is not controversial and looking at the payment record seems like a reasonable approach, the possibility of resentment at this point is minimal.

2. The first sentence is designed to open the mind for discussion; a refusal stated in the first sentence could have closed it. Discussion of the purchase-and-payment record is based on facts that are verifiable. That a clerk could in the haste of a busy day transpose a figure is understandable. That a customer is accountable for payment of purchases made is reasonable.
3. The reasons-first sequence gives reasons the emphasis they deserve.
4. In view of the reasons given, the sentence that conveys the refusal may not be resented at all. Just as "It isn't fair" is a likely reaction to a refusal stated in the first sentence. "It seems logical" is a likely reaction to a refusal preceded by good explanations.
5. Since the last sentence is not about the refusal, the negative is de-emphasized.

The reasons-before-refusal sequence has a possible disadvantage: Because the main point is delayed until late in the letter, some readers may become impatient; that's not good. But if the main point is presented first, some readers may become angry; that's worse. Best way to reduce the impact of impatience: Have good reasons and present them concisely.

Letters that present negative thoughts are written persuasively, designed to get a reader to accept a point of view. Likewise, letters designed to get a reader to do something or to buy something are written persuasively.

When the reader will not be interested initially. When readers receive sales letters or letters requesting special favors, their minds are probably on other matters. Being neither pleased, displeased, nor interested, they will have to be made interested and persuaded.

Naturally, a first sentence that says "Send $150 and I will send you a . . ." or "Will you please donate 45 hours of your spare time" is likely to get a negative reaction. The following sequence of ideas is recommended for letters in which the reader will not be interested:

1. Say something to get attention—to make the recipient put aside other thoughts and concentrate on this letter.
2. Introduce the product or idea.
3. Give enough evidence to demonstrate that accepting the proposal would be to the recipient's advantage.

4. Encourage the action necessary for gaining the benefits described.

The advantages of this sequence, and examples of application, are shown in Chapter 8.

The sequence-of-idea patterns presented in this chapter are recommended for *most* correspondence. The outlines are presented as useful *guides* that will help to get the composition started and give the writer confidence that a sensible plan is being followed. They are not to be thought of as *rules* from which there can be no deviation. They are to be thought of as techniques that will help to achieve the twin purposes of clarity and harmony.

When special circumstances indicate that deviation from the guides would best serve the purpose of the writer, that deviation is certainly justified. For example, if a request is resubmitted after an inductive denial, a deductive denial may provide the needed emphasis in the second denial. Or, if a reader is known to *prefer* main-idea-first sequence in all messages, a deductive denial is acceptable. Having a set of guides from which there can be occasional deviation seems much better than having no guides at all.

Getting ready to write is just as important as the writing itself. What is the purpose? What is the message? What will be the reaction to it? What is the best sequence of ideas? All these questions should be answered before the writing is begun.

SUMMARY

Success in writing a letter is closely associated with the planning that precedes. The task of composition should not be undertaken until the following questions have been answered: (1) Is the letter designed to convey the right message? (2) Is the letter being written for the right purpose? (3) Is the letter likely to evoke an emotional reaction? (4) Should the sequence be inductive or deductive? The answer to the fourth question depends on the answer to the third.

Readers can be expected to react in one of four ways: (1) *pleased,* (2) *interested* but not emotionally involved, (3) *displeased,* or (4) initially *not interested.* For the first two reactions, a deductive approach is recommended; for the other reactions, an inductive approach is recommended.

When readers will be pleased, the following outline is recommended:

begin with the most pleasant aspect of the letter, follow with details, and close with a sentence that either reminds the reader of the pleasant thought or looks positively to the future. This technique places emphasis on the positive, puts the reader immediately in a pleasant mood, and gets the writer off to a fast start.

When readers will be merely interested but not emotionally involved, the outline is likewise deductive: put the main idea first, follow with details, and close with a reference to the main idea or to action that is to be taken.

When readers will be displeased with the basic message, the following outline is recommended: begin with a pleasant or neutral statement that leads to a discussion of reasons, present facts and supporting reasons, state the unpleasant idea, and close with a positive or neutral statement. This technique allows the writer to present reasons in an emphatic position. Having first seen the logic of the reasons, readers are less likely to react negatively when the disappointing idea is presented.

When readers will not be interested initially, the recommended outline is inductive: get attention, introduce the idea or product, present evidence, and ask for action. Such an outline allows a reader to see advantages of taking action before being asked to act.

Good composition is preceded by careful planning.

Chapter 6

WRITING ABOUT THE ROUTINE AND THE PLEASANT

Recall from the preceding chapter that two questions must be answered before the writing is begun: (1) Exactly, what is the message? (2) What is the receiver's expected reaction?

Recall, too, that the receiver's reaction will fall into one of the following categories: (1) pleased, (2) displeased, (3) neither pleased nor displeased but interested, and (4) not initially interested. This chapter is devoted to a further discussion of letters in the first and third categories. Letters in the first group are referred to as "yes" letters, letters in the third as "routine" letters.

"Yes" and "routine" letters are discussed in the same chapter because both follow the same sequence-of-idea pattern:

1. Pleasant idea in a "yes" letter or main idea in a "routine" letter.
2. Details or explanations.
3. Closing thought.

The preceding outline is deductive—major idea first, followed by supporting details. Item 3 could be omitted without seriously impairing effectiveness, but including it gives a letter the quality of unity and avoids abruptness.

For "yes" and "routine" letters, the deductive sequence has several advantages: (1) The first sentence can be dictated with very little hesitation; once past the first sentence, writers can follow easily with details. (2) The first sentence attracts attention; raders know immediately what the message is. (3) When the first sentence says "yes," readers are put in a pleasant frame of mind right at the start; in this state, they are receptive to the details that follow. (4) Readers' time may be saved; having received the good news or the big idea, they can move rapidly through the supporting detail.

This basic plan is applicable in several business-writing problems: claim letters, credit letters, order letters, and request letters.

CLAIM LETTERS

A claim letter is a request for an adjustment. When writers ask for something to which they think they are entitled (refund, replacement, exchange, payment for damages, and so forth), the letter is called a "claim" letter. These letters can be divided into two groups: *routine* claims and *persuasive* claims. The latter (discussed in a later chapter) assume the request will be granted only after explanations and persuasive arguments have been presented. The former (because of guarantees, warranties, or other contractual conditions) assume the request will be granted quickly and willingly, without persuasion. When the claim is routine (when a direct statement of the desired action is not likely to meet resistance), the deductive approach is employed:

Gentlemen

Please send a new garden hose to replace the one I am returning to Woods-Edwards today.

Reveals the claim in the first sentence and thus saves time.

Although our water pressure is 10 pounds less than the 50-pound limit mentioned in the guarantee, this hose split after two weeks' use.

Gives supporting details.

I shall appreciate your returning the new hose as soon as you can.

Ends with a polite, confident reference to the action desired.

The same sequence of ideas is recommended for "yes" replies to routine claim letters: good news (customer is getting what was requested) stated in the first sentence.

Businesses *want* their customers to write (or call) when merchandise or service is not satisfactory. They want to learn of ways in which goods and services can be improved, and they want to see that their customers get value received for the money they spend. Typically, customers will take time to write only if they think their claims are legitimate.

After having said "yes" in the very first sentence, we can't stop there. The request was made because something went wrong, and for whatever went wrong there must be a reason. We have to explain it. Otherwise, the client may assume that we have no explanation or that such problems are frequent in our business. If the claim clearly resulted from our own mistake, we should admit it frankly. Most people like to do business with others who have the courage to admit it when they make a mistake. If we grant a claim in spite of the customer's fault, we must explain it; otherwise, the same problem may present itself again.

We can actually build business with our adjustment letters. By making things right and explaining why they went wrong, we can gain a reputation as a business that stands behind its goods or services. A loyal customer may be even more loyal after a business has demonstrated its integrity.

The "yes" adjustment letter can actually work for us as a low-pressure sales letter. Since we are writing about our product or service, we have the opportunity to speak of it in a favorable light—to reassure the client that the choice is actually a good one. (Such reassurance is known as "resale.") In addition, we may be able to generate interest in some related item. (Introducing a related item or service is known as using "sales-promotional material.") We can be reasonably sure that such resale and sales-promotional material will be read. We don't have that assurance when we send sales letters.

Sometimes the adjustment department decides to grant some claims even though it has sufficient evidence to warrant refusal. But saying "We're granting your request but we don't have to do so" can do as much to destroy the business relationship as would a direct refusal. Notice how the following letter says "yes" but also lets the customer know what can be done to prevent recurrence of the problem:

Mrs. West

Two long-lasting, snow-white Dresso shirts are on their way to you. Your account will not be charged.

Grants request. Puts customer in good frame of mind for understanding the remainder of the letter. Includes some resale on the shirts.

Compared with conventional shirts, Dresso wash-and-wears stay whiter, last longer, and remain more wrinkle free.

Reassures the housewife that she made a wise choice when she chose wash-and-wears, and leads into an explanation of how to get maximum results.

But for maximum service, they must be washed by hand without strong bleaches.

Uses the shirts (instead of the addressee) as subject of this sentence because it treats a negative idea. She will probably recall that she has not been washing them or having them washed by hand. Through positive language, she is made to see her mistake.

When you take them to your laundryman, just ask him to follow the washing instructions that we have placed on the collar label.

Presents a suggestion that will prevent future trouble. Refers unaccusingly to the laundry label, which has evidently been disregarded.

You should receive our annual clearance-sale catalogue within a few days.

Reminds Mrs. West that we still expect her to order merchandise from us.

Notice that the preceding letter grants a request, but it does not employ the word *grant*. And it does not refer to the letter being answered as a *claim*. Although these words are convenient in talking *about* such letters, they are not good words to use *in* such letters. "We are *granting* your request" can also convey "We see ourselves as being in a position of power" or "We are acceding to your unjustified request." "We are adjusting your *claim*" can also convey "We are responding to your overly strong statement of dissatisfaction."

Confident that a routine request for an adjustment will be granted, a writer simply asks for it (in the first sentence and without seeming to complain). Knowing that the recipient will be glad to learn that a request has been granted, a writer simply states it (in the first sentence and without apparent reluctance). The details and closing sentence follow naturally and easily.

CREDIT LETTERS

The network of credit associations across the country has made knowledge about individual consumers easily obtainable. As a result, exchanges of credit information are common in business. Normally, credit information is requested and transmitted by form letters or simple office forms. Like claim and adjustment letters, they present the main point first:

Gentlemen

May we have credit information about Mr. William F. Frame? He has applied for credit with us and has given your business as a reference.

Quickly reveals the nature of the request and the name of the person.

After filling in the blanks on this page, use the back side for additional remarks if necessary. Your reply will be held in strict confidence.

Gives assurance that the information will be used for authorized purposes only.

Length of time sold on credit ______________________________
Highest credit extended ______________________________
Credit limit ______________________________
Balance now due __________ Balance past due ______________
Normal paying habits ______________________________
Remarks ______________________________
____

Asks for the specific information needed.

Thank you for your help. Please call or write to us when we can be of similar assistance.

Ends courteously.

Another good arrangement for a credit request is to place the complete letter at the top of the page and to arrange the fill-in items at the bottom of the page. If a subject line is used, the letter can be even shorter than the preceding example. Printed forms on which the name of the reference and applicant can be written are certainly desirable when the volume of credit requests is great.

Replies to requests for credit information are usually very simple—just fill in the blanks and return it. If the request does not include a form, follow a deductive plan in writing:

We considered Mr. William F. Frame, about whom you requested confidential credit information on May 26, as a very good credit risk.

Presents major idea. Confirms confidential nature of the information.

During the ten years in which we sold building materials to him on credit, his highest balance was $50,000. His payments were always prompt. He reduced his balance to zero before moving away from Spring City.

Gives details requested.

Mr. Frame was a pleasant person with whom to transact business.

Ends on a pleasant note.

In such letters, writers have an obligation to themselves, as well as to the addressee and the credit applicant. Presenting factual information is better than making statements that seem to be promises. "His payments were always prompt" sounds more objective than "I'm sure he will pay promptly." "He *paid* us regularly" seems more believable than "He *will pay* you regularly."

When would-be purchasers want to begin buying on credit and assume credit will be granted willingly, they should present the main point quickly:

Will you please fill the enclosed order on a credit basis.

Presents the major idea.

If you need information other than that given on the enclosed financial statements, please write to me.

Alludes to supporting details.

I plan to place a similar order every two weeks.

Closes with a look to the future.

This approach is recommended only when the writer's supporting financial statements are assumed sufficient to merit a "yes" response.

Before replying to requests for credit, managers seek information from such sources as (1) the potential customer, (2) credit-rating associations, (3) other businesses, and (4) other people who may have some knowledge of the potential customer's paying habits. Satisfied that the applicant will have the money and the willingness to pay when the debt is due, the typical credit manager sends a form letter.

Form letters are used because firms receive so many credit requests that the cost of individualized letters would be prohibitive. Individualized letters do a better job of promoting sales and goodwill. Whether to say "yes" by form letter or by individualized letter is a problem that each credit manager must answer. If the list of credit customers is short and few names are being added, individualized letters may be more practical. Regardless of whether the credit-granting letter is a form letter, the get-right-to-the-point sequence is recommended:

1. Begin by saying credit terms have been arranged; or, if an order has been placed, begin by telling of the shipment of goods and thus implying the credit grant.
2. Reveal the basis for the credit grant.
3. Present and explain the credit terms.
4. Include some resale or sales-promotional material.
5. End with a confident look toward future business.

Revealing the basis for credit may help to prevent collection problems that could arise later. A reminder that credit has been established on the basis of prompt-pay habits is an inducement to continue those habits.

Presenting and explaining the credit terms may also help to prevent collection problems that could arise later. If customers know exactly when payments are expected, payments are more likely to be prompt. If customers know exactly how discount terms are calculated, excessive discounts (and resulting correspondence) are less likely. The mere fact that terms are discussed in detail implies that terms are important, that they are to be followed. Notice the application of these principles in the following letter:

Mr. Cook

The easy-to-display adjustable screwdrivers should reach your store in time for your weekend shoppers.

Presents good news. Reminds the dealer of an important advantage in stocking this particular screwdriver. Indicates that the writer has some consideration for the problems of a dealer. Implies the credit grant.

Pay us later.

States specifically that credit has been granted. Leads to an explanation of the basis and terms of the credit arrangement.

Because of your very favorable current ratio and your prompt-pay habits with your other creditors, we are sending the shipment subject to the usual credit terms—2/10, n 30.

Gives the dealer recognition for having earned the credit privilege. Reminds him there is a reason for his credit grant. Introduces the credit terms.

By paying this invoice within 10 days, you save almost a dollar—about enough to equal the markup on two screwdriver sales.

Encourages the dealer's taking advantage of the discount.

By using the display rod included with the shipment, you can save counter space and still be assured that your customer will see these handy screwdrivers.

Presents additional resale.

For other hardware items on open account, here is a handy order form.

Looks confidently forward to future orders.

The preceding letter performed two functions; it said "yes" to an application for credit and it also said "Yes, your order is being filled." The credit aspect was emphasized more than the acknowledgment. But when the order is for cash, or when credit terms have been arranged already, the primary purpose may be to acknowledge an order.

ORDER LETTERS

Order letters create one half of a contract—the "offer" portion. By sending the goods, the shipper completes the other half—the "acceptance" portion. Therefore, one who wants to receive merchandise should use direct language; the order letter should be a definite offer. The recommended sequence for ideas in an order letter:

1. Present the order in the first sentence. Use specific language; such as, "Please ship," "please send," or "I order." Avoid phrases like "I am interested in ordering," "I would like to order," or similar indefinite statements.
2. Carefully detail the items ordered. Be specific by mentioning catalog numbers, prices, colors, sizes, and all other information that will enable the seller to fill the order promptly and without the need for further correspondence.

3. Include payment plan (or payment) and shipping instructions. Remember that the shipper is free to ship by the normal method in the absence of specific instructions from the buyer. Tell when, where, and how the order is to be shipped.
4. Close the letter with a confident expectation of delivery.

In addition to the application of the outline principles, notice the physical arrangement of the following order letter:

Gentlemen

Please ship me the following items, which are listed in your current winter catalog:

24	#2314 Black record Tower type-writer ribbons @ 4.00	$ 96.00
100	#2332 8½ x 13 Bristol file dividers @ .43	43.00
12	#2408 Stick-type erasers with attached brush @ .44	5.28
		$144.28

The enclosed check for $166.00 covers the $16.00 parcel post charge and local sales tax of $5.72. I shall appreciate receiving the materials by April 8.

If the preceding letter had not included payment, it should have mentioned the plan by which payment was to be made. If credit had not been established, financial information should have been included. If an order form is available, an order letter may not be necessary. Sometimes a short letter is sent with the order form. The letter introduces the order form and provides information not called for on the form.

When customers place orders for merchandise, they expect to get exactly what they ordered; and they want it quickly. Most orders are acknowledged by shipment. No letter is necessary. But for initial orders or for orders that cannot be filled quickly and precisely, an acknowledgment should be sent. Senders of initial orders like to know that they are going to receive what they ordered; they like to know their business is appreciated; they appreciate information about the firm with which they are beginning a business relationship. And if old customers' orders are not being filled immediately, they have a right to some form of explanation. It is usually a duplicated or printed sheet that says something like:

> Dear Customer
>
> We appreciate your order for ____________________.
> It will be shipped within ______days.
>
> Cordially

Such forms are often sent as a matter of routine when orders can be filled immediately but will require considerable time in transit.

Although such a form is impersonal, it is appreciated because it acknowledges the order and lets the customer have some idea of its disposition. But other-than-routine acknowledgments require an individualized letter. Although initial orders can be acknowledged through form letters, the letters are more effective if individually dictated.

A primary purpose of the acknowledgment letter is to encourage future business. A good way to achieve this goal is to (1) send what was ordered, (2) generate some awareness of its good qualities, and (3) convey the message that future orders will be handled in the same efficient manner. But future business can hardly be encouraged by use of the words "welcome" and "gratitude" when actions are not consistent with these words. Those whose merchandise and service are poor overwork these words.

REQUEST LETTERS

Businesses send many letters requesting information about people, prices, products, and services. Because such requests are door-openers for further business, readers accept them optimistically; but at the same time, they draw opinions about the writer based on the quality of the letter. The following outline can serve as a guide in the preparation of effective requests that are expected to be fulfilled:

1. Make the major request in the first sentence. Use a subject line if the letter lends itself to one.
2. Follow the major request with the details that will make the request clear. If possible, use tabulations.
3. Close with a forward look to the reader's next step.

This outline is employed in the following letter:

Will you please tell me who made the small Japanese-type lanterns you have recently placed near the entrance to Cartwright Park.

I think the small ones (about 1½ feet high with a wide top and small base) would fit very well into my landscaping pattern.

I shall appreciate you sending me the name and address of their manufacturer.

The letter is short; but, if it conveys enough information and has a tone of politeness, it is long enough. The following simple request is long enough; it needs no embellishment:

Gentlemen

Please send me a copy of your latest price list. I am especially interested in R. D. Irwin's textbooks in management.

Cordially

Letters that say "yes" to requests are usually very easy to write because no resistance is expected. Notice that the following letter employs the same pattern recommended for other routine and "yes" letters:

Mr. Worth

Yes, our Suggestions Supervisor, Mr. Rudolph Smith, can talk with you from 1:30 to 2:00 on November 20.

After he leaves for his two o'clock meeting, you may enjoy looking through our files of accepted and rejected suggestions. Mr. Smith thinks they will be of special interest to you, since you are doing a thesis on suggestion plans.

After you have finished compiling the results of your study, we would like to see them.

Cordially

This letter (and all letters discussed in this chapter) introduces the main point in the very first sentence. Details follow. But some letters (discussed in the next chapter) cannot profitably employ that sequence.

SUMMARY

If a letter conveys routine information, a reader is not likely to be involved emotionally. The reaction is neither happiness nor unhappiness. In this category of reader reaction are claim letters that are highly likely to get what is asked for, ordinary requests for credit information, order letters, and request letters. All letters in this category (1) begin with the main idea, (2) follow with details, and (3) close with a reference to desired action or a look to the future.

Similarly, favorable replies to such letters follow a deductive pattern: (1) begin with the "yes" response, (2) follow with details, (3) include an appropriate, forward-looking closing or a reference to the main (pleasant) idea.

From the writer's point of view, this sequence-of-idea pattern provides a dependable way of getting a letter started. Once the main idea has been presented in the first sentence, following with the remainder of the letter is easy. From the reader's point of view, the pattern saves time and (by getting right to the point) emphasizes the point that most deserves emphasis.

Chapter 7

WRITING ABOUT THE UNPLEASANT

Before the writing is begun, two questions must be answered: (1) What, exactly, is the message? (2) What is the most likely reader reaction? When the message is unpleasant (a "no" answer to a request, for example), the reaction is likely to be one of disappointment. The writer's goal is to convey the message and to minimize the disappointment.

If the sentence that contains the disappointing idea should come at the beginning, the unpleasant idea receives emphasis. Holding goodwill (promoting business harmony) is difficult when emphasis is placed on negatives. Therefore, the following sequence-of-idea pattern is recommended:

1. Neutral statement that leads to reasons.
2. Facts, analysis, reasons.

3. Unpleasant message.
4. A related idea that takes emphasis away from the unpleasant.

Notice that the reasons *precede* the statement of the unpleasant.

When we say "no," we should have a reason to support it. We assume our reader is a reasonable person. Having been led to understand the reasons, the reader may agree that the request should have been denied.

No one has a foolproof formula for persuading readers to agree that their requests should have been refused. Remember, though, that the recipient is entitled to an explanation for refusal. Presenting the refusal *before* presenting the explanation has two disadvantages: (1) The reader may stop before reading the explanation. (2) After having received a disappointment, the reader's mind may not be receptive to an explanation.

Presenting reasons first provides an effective technique for emphasizing reasons (explanations). The more clearly readers understand good reasons, the less the feeling of disappointment when the unpleasant idea is stated. Naturally, good letter planning and writing can hardly be expected to make readers just as happy with refusals as they would have been with acceptances. Rather, the goal is to get readers to *understand* reasons. The more clearly they understand them the less the likelihood that they will think the decision is illogical, unfair, or arbitrary.

Presenting reasons first has a possible disadvantage, however. If the reasons should be presented in a long, involved, round-about way, readers may become impatient before the unpleasant idea is stated. Therefore, the reasons should be stated vividly and concisely. If they are, the reader can concentrate on them.

Well-written explanations (reasons) that precede refusals are unlikely to cause a feeling of impatience as the explanations are being read. Even if they should cause impatience, consider these alternatives: (1) While reading the preliminary explanations, readers become a little impatient. (2) After reading the refusal in the first sentence, readers have a feeling that trying to understand the reasons is pointless or that they should concentrate on rebuttal as they read. The latter alternative seems much more damaging.

The sequence-of-idea pattern suggested in this chapter is not intended as the pattern to be used in every refusal-type letter. Sometimes, circumstances are such that a writer may actually *want* to jolt the reader with an emphasized refusal followed by a subordinated explanation. If doing so conveys the message adequately and promotes the kind of reader-writer relationship desired, the procedure is acceptable. But, before taking that approach, a writer should give serious thought to the reaction it will produce.

ADJUSTMENT REFUSALS

When business prudence dictates that we should say "no," the major writing problems are (1) saying "no" as inoffensively as possible and (2) presenting supporting reasons as convincingly as possible.

The following letter refuses a request for replacement of an electric blanket. The recipient had received the blanket as a gift and had left if in storage for about three years while he was out of the country. After only a few weeks of use, it failed to function. Recalling that the blanket had a two-year warranty (and not recalling that it was for two years from purchase date instead of two years of use), the user returned the blanket to the manufacturer and asked for a replacement.

Mrs. Smith

From the sewn-in label on the blanket you returned to us, we see that it was manufactured at our East Coast factory in 1979.

Reveals that this letter is about the blanket that was returned, but neither gives a "no" answer nor leads the reader to expect a "yes" answer. Leads into explanations.

Attached to the label at the time of sale were instructions for cleaning and drying and a warranty that extended two years from date of purchase. The purchaser's warranty form shows December 13, 1979, as the date of purchase. Materials and workmanship were guaranteed until December 13, 1981 (18 months ago).

Because the wiring in electric blankets is necessarily delicate, the instructions stated that (after being washed) the blanket was to be dried by hanging on a line. Its present condition suggests that it was put through some type of wringing process, which explains the malfunction.

Presents the reasons that support the upcoming refusal.

If the blanket had been subjected to the type of drying process recommended, and if it had been returned within two years from the purchase date, it would have been replaced at no charge.

> *Conveys the refusal. By revealing what would have been done if conditions had been different, the sentence reveals the refusal. This technique (subjunctive statement) enables the writer to reveal the refusal in language that is positive. But if such a refusal statement seems too subtle, if a more direct refusal seems desirable, negative language can be used.*

The blanket is not being replaced because drying instructions were not followed and because the warranty period has expired.

> *To keep the negative from sounding any more forceful than necessary, the sentence uses the blanket (instead of Ms. Smith) as the subject; it also uses passive voice.*

Made of heavy-weight material, it is still a useful cover and is being returned to you today.

For our most recent innovations in woolen and synthetic materials, see pages 4 through 7 of the booklet that is being sent to you.

> *Closes on a topic that is about something other than the refusal. Such a closing helps take emphasis off the refusal and implies future transactions.*

The preceding letter illustrates the inductive refusal; it seeks to emphasize the reasons and subordinate the statement of refusal. It illustrates techniques that are recommended. But, for refusal writing in general, here are some techniques to be avoided:

1. Beginning by talking about something only remotely related to the subject of the letter. (If the preceding letter had—in an attempt to begin on a neutral point—begun with "The enclosed brochure shows our latest blankets," the reader would have been led to expect a sales message instead of a letter about the blanket returned.)
2. Giving an elementary lecture. "If a business is to continue, it must formulate and follow plans."
3. Recalling the original disappointment too vividly. "We know how you must have felt when the blanket failed to heat," would have come as an unneeded reminder of the unpleasant; and it might have caused the reader to expect a "yes" answer.

4. Employing strong resale in the beginning. "The blanket you returned was one of the very best we manufacture" might (at the moment it is read) generate some negative thoughts that will interfere with concentration on the upcoming reasons. Suggesting that the blanket is good when at the moment the recipient thinks of evidence to the contrary is risking disagreement at the very beginning.
5. Prolonging the explanations. Unnecessarily long explanations will add to any impatience that may exist.
6. Presenting explanations that are so short or general as to be unconvincing. We should give enough detail to make the reasons clear.
7. Hiding behind "company policy." From experience, many will think of "company policy" as something to hide behind, as a standard answer that is easy to give and not to be challenged.
8. Seeming to accuse. When we want to remind someone of his mistake, we can usually employ third person, impersonal language, and passive construction to get the point across in an inoffensive way.
9. Employing too much negative language. The following words and expressions can be especially annoying: amazed, cannot understand, claim, damage, defective, delay, dissatisfied, error, fault, inconvenience, regret, shocked, surprised, unfortunately, you evidently, you should have, you failed, wrong.
10. Using a tone that hints of "bending over backward" or "giving blood" when offering a counter proposal. Offer it willingly or not at all.
11. Closing by revealing doubts about whether the explanation will be accepted. "We trust this is satisfactory" suggests "We ourselves doubt whether we have made the right business decision or presented it in the right way."
12. Apologizing for action taken. We should take a course of action only when we have a good reason for doing so; therefore, it is inconsistent to end by saying, "We're sorry we had to refuse." Rather, we should be glad to stand behind our reasons.
13. Closing with a reminder of future trouble. "When this happens again, just. . . ." ends a letter with an unpleasant, negative thought.
14. Closing with a meaningless, outworn expression. "Thank you for your interest" adds very little to a message.

15. Inviting a prolonged correspondence. "If you have any further questions, please don't hesitate to write" indicates that the case is still open, that pertinent information may not have been considered, and that through further correspondence the decision may be reversed.
16. Closing on an ironic note. "When we can be of *further* help, please call on us" may be intended to reveal a helpful attitude; but such an ending is especially bitter when the extent of our helpfulness has been to say "no." The sentence could be taken to mean "When you want another refusal, just write."

The principles employed in adjustment refusal are similar to principles employed in other refusals. The techniques to avoid are likewise similar.

CREDIT REFUSALS

Once we have evaluated a request for credit and have decided "no" is the right answer, our primary writing problem is to say "no" so tactfully that we keep the business relationship on a cash basis. Since requests for credit are often accompanied with an order, our credit refusals may serve as acknowledgment letters. And every business letter is directly or indirectly a sales letter. Our prospective customer may be disappointed when he cannot buy on a credit basis; but if we keep him sold on our goods and services, he may prefer to buy from us on a cash basis instead of seeking credit privileges elsewhere.

In credit refusals, as in other types of refusals, the major portion of the message should be explanation. We cannot expect our readers to agree that our "no" answers are the right answers unless we give the reasons behind them. Naturally, those who send us credit information will expect us to keep it confidential. But if we give the reasons without using the names of those from whom we obtained our information, we are not violating confidence. We are passing along the truth as a justification for our business decisions. Both writers and readers benefit from the explanation of the reasons behind the refusal. For writers, the explanation helps to establish fair-mindedness; it shows they are businesslike, that the decision was not arbitrary. For readers, the explanation not only presents the truth to which they are entitled; it has guidance value. From it they may learn to adjust habits and as a result qualify for credit purchases later.

Notice that the following credit refusal presents reasons first and that its author incorporates salesmanship:

Mr. Dobson

Because of the current advertising in *Wife* and *Leader's* magazines, Sporta Tuna is fast becoming the best-selling tuna.

Implies receipt of the order. Lets the grocer know this is a response to the order and credit request, and at the same time confirms his choice. The reminder of the National advertising may make him want to buy Sporta even if he cannot buy it on a credit basis.

First-time orders such as yours are coming in daily.

Provides a little more resale and leads into the explanation of refusal.

Thank you for the list of wholesalers from whom you have been making credit purchases.

Suggests a tone of friendliness by indicating, in a natural way, that his thoughtfulness in enclosing the list is appreciated. Provides a transition from the resale beginning into an explanation.

Although your Dun and Bradstreet rating is perfectly satisfactory, some of the referents reported that your recent payments have been as much as 90 days overdue.

Presents reasons before the "no" answer and removes a little of the sting from the adverse reports by preceding them with the favorable report. The technique suggests fair-mindedness on the part of the writer. He considers both the good and the bad. To have mentioned the names of references would have been a violation of confidence.

Of course, we know this circumstance could be a temporary condition for which you have a good explanation.

Maintains a positive tone. Leads to request for explanation.

So we may supply you with time shipments of choice quality tuna while current national advertising is in full swing, may we have your explanation?

Recognizes that every story has two sides. Further indicates fair-mindedness. Sounds confident of—but does not promise—future credit transactions. Induces the recipient to send the explanation by reminding him of the advantages in selling Sporta.

Or, may we have permission to ship Sporta by sight draft with bill of lading attached?

Presents an alternative proposal. The "sight draft with bill of lading attached" is tantamount to a cash transaction, since a local bank will make the collection before the tuna is delivered.

Our cash terms are 2/10, n/30.

Presents cash terms as an introduction to the advantages in buying on a cash basis.

At $28.00 per case, your cash discount on 12 cases amounts to $6.90—an amount about equal to your markup on one case.

Seeks to be convincing by presenting concrete figures. The fact that the writer takes time for calculation illustrates his desire to be helpful.

In addition to the national advertising, the 24 per cent markup is a major reason for choosing Sporta tuna.

Re-emphasizes the advantages of stocking Sporta—a further inducement to accept the invitation to buy for cash.

May we have your instructions right away, so that you can supply your customers with choice quality Sporta while the demand is high.

Ends with a request for action. Uses the general word "Instructions" because the reader may choose to cancel, write an explanation, or wire instructions to ship sight draft with bill of lading attached. Gives final reminder that there is an advantage in stocking Sporta now. That reminder is itself an inducement to action.

A disadvantage of the preceding letter is that it is longer, requires more thought, and is more costly than a short, abrupt refusal. But if it is the beginning of a long business relationship, it is well worth the price.

ORDER REFUSALS

If a customer orders directly from a manufacturer who sells only through distributors, the order is refused. Notice the similarity between order refusals and other types of refusals.

Mr. Estman

The seat covers you ordered directly from us are made of Miraplast plastic.

Implies receipt of the order; leads to a suggestion that the purchaser has made a good choice.

Miraplast looks like good-quality gingham—feels almost like it, too; but it is so durable that we have asked our dealers to extend the guarantee to two years instead of one.

Gives a little more detail about the outstanding qualities; doing so increases the chances of getting the customer to buy from a dealer. Introduces dealers before indicating that purchases must be made through them.

To give our plastic users a wider selection of materials and fast, free installation, we market Miraplast through dealers only.

Presents the reasons for marketing through dealers, then follows logically with the information that sales are not made directly to consumers. This negative thought is expressed in positive language.

The address of your nearest dealer is given at the bottom of this page. By calling at that address, you get a plastic that fits perfectly—plastic that lasts and lasts.

Refers to the action the customer is to take. Encourages action by reminding the customer of the reward for taking it.

If such letters are sent frequently, form letters are satisfactory and inexpensive.

Because of sellers' experience with certain products, they may be better informed about buyers' needs than are the buyers themselves. If a buyer orders a product that the seller knows will be unsatisfactory for that buyer's needs, the order should be refused. Like other refusal letters, reasons would precede the refusal. If the seller does stock what is *needed,* the letter would first acknowledge the order, explain why the item *ordered* would be unsatisfactory, and ask for further instructions. By pointing out virtues of the item needed, the writer encourages authorization to ship it instead of the item originally ordered.

When an order is received for merchandise that is not stocked, it should be returned:

Foreign Models Incorporated handles carburetors and other parts for European cars only.

If you will place your order (which we are returning) with the firm listed at the bottom of this page, you should have your carburetor within a short time.

When you need to trade cars, come in and see our selections. We sell 12 different makes—from low-priced economy cars to the most expensive European sports cars.

Telling the customer where the merchandise *can* be purchased is a polite gesture. Including some sales promotional material is an inexpensive way to advertise. The letter is almost sure to be read—something we can't say of all sales messages.

FAVOR REFUSALS

Every business person will at some time be asked for a favor—a contribution for which there will be little or no reward. The following letter rejects a fraternity's request for permission to take some rocks from a right-of-way:

Mr. Woods

The rocks on the Turnpike right-of-way were left there at the suggestion of Commission engineers.

Employs a neutral beginning, which identifies the subject of the letter and leads into a discussion of the reasons behind the refusal.

When the Turnpike was completed, the Commission had plans for future drainage improvement and repair.

Reveals the purpose for which the rocks are to be used.

They foresaw that some rocks on the right-of-way would be useful when flash floods hit the drainage ditches in the Kaywood area.

Presents the specific reasons for the rocks and leads the receiver to expect the refusal that follows.

Since the last three years have been very dry, little repair work has been necessary; but we think we should keep the rocks as insurance against heavy spring rains, which occasionally come to this area.

Leads from the reasons into a statement of refusal. Employs a long, complex sentence to de-emphasize the negative.

For your construction purposes, maybe you could use a different material or a different source. Regardless of the question, someone in the fraternity will come forth with a good answer.

Closes on a topic other than the refusal itself.

From the preceding letters, we can see that all "no" letters have several characteristics in common. Adjustment refusals, credit refusals, order refusals, favor refusals—they all follow the same basic plan: (1) They begin with a neutral or agreement-getting beginning. (2) They present reasons behind a refusal before presenting the refusal. (3) They present the refusal without emphasizing it. (4) They include an alternative if appropriate. (5) They end on a pleasant or neutral note.

SUMMARY

If a refusal is conveyed in the very first sentence of a letter, a reader may not bother to read explanations that follow or disappointment may be so strong that the reader concentrates on rebuttal (instead of understanding) while the explanations are being read. Because the explanations are important, a writer should present them in a position in which they are most likely to be read and understood. If that goal is achieved, the disappointment may be either diminished or eliminated. Therefore, the following sequence-of-idea pattern is recommended for letters that convey disappointing information: begin with a neutral statement that leads to reasons, present explanations and reasons, then present the unpleasant idea, and follow with a related idea that takes emphasis away from the unpleasant. The same basic pattern is recommended for adjustment refusals, credit refusals, order refusals, and favor refusals.

Chapter 8

WRITING TO PERSUADE

The letters discussed in preceding chapters were designed (1) to convey information or (2) to get action. Some were designed for both. Letters in this chapter are designed to get action, but they differ from previously discussed action-getting letters. The difference results from the circumstances surrounding the action desired.

In letters about orders, requests for information, and requests for adjustments, the assumption was that the reader would be willing to take the desired action once it was identified. For example, a supplier who has by mistake shipped the wrong merchandise would almost certainly want to correct the error when attention is directed to it. Circumstances are such that telling *why* the correction should be made is hardly necessary.

Sometimes, however, we must ask for action when circumstances are such that the proposal will probably be rejected unless we do show *why* it should be accepted. For example, we could hardly expect people to accept our proposal that they buy a product if our letter did not reveal *why* doing so would be beneficial. We could hardly expect business executives to provide classified information about their businesses without some preliminary explanation and assurance. Under such conditions, letters have to be persuasive. They have to provide readers with information sufficient to make them want to take the action desired.

Persuasive letters, then, are *sales* letters. They *sell* the idea that one should buy a product or take some other type of action. For various reasons, readers can be expected to resist taking the action desired:

1. Their minds (at the time of exposure to the letter) are on some other problem. They may be reluctant to dismiss it long enough to consider the proposal. They may not have been expecting to receive *this* message. In fact, they may at the moment be disappointed because what they consider a more important message is not in today's mail. Therefore, the very first sentence will have to succeed in *getting attention,* in generating willingness to read.

2. They may have sensed no need for (or interest in) the proposal. They may be perfectly satisfied with circumstances as they are. A new idea that would require changes in routines, a new product when an old one is apparently satisfactory—these thoughts may be distasteful. Therefore, the first sentences must have an interesting way of *introducing the proposal.*

3. They may resist (or choose to ignore) supporting evidence. They may not care about the proposal. After all, it belongs to someone else; considering it may be damaging to the ego. They may have considered the proposal (or a similar one) previously and already made up their minds. Additional facts may not be appreciated. They are probably interested in the proposal only if they can identify specific reasons why acceptance would be beneficial to them. Unsupported generalizations and high-pressure talk will almost surely be unacceptable as valid reasons for doing what is asked. Therefore, the sales letter must concentrate on *providing sufficient evidence* to convince readers of the proposal's merits.

4. They may agree that the proposal is good but choose to ignore it. They may be habitual procrastinators, or just plain lazy. They may not do what is wanted unless they are told exactly what to do. Therefore, the sales message closes by *encouraging action* on the part of the reader.

The sequence of ideas in good-news and routine letters is deductive, but the sequence in persuasive letters is inductive—getting attention, introducing the proposal, providing sufficient evidence, and encouraging action. But before the writing is begun, writers can profitably take into account certain considerations peculiar to the writing of sales messages.

BEFORE THE WRITING

As preliminary steps to sales-letter composition, writers need to know (1) the product and how it differs from competing products, (2) something about the people to whom letters are to be directed, (3) the specific action desired, and (4) some basic principles of sales-letter composition.

The product and how it differs. Writers of effective sales letters are not satisfied to know their products in a general way; they want the details. They get such details by (1) reading all available literature, (2) using the product and comparing it with others, (3) conducting tests and experiments, (4) watching others use the product, (5) observing the manufacturing process, and (6) soliciting reports from users. Before they can write, they need concrete answers to such questions as these:

What will the product do for people?
From what materials is it made?
By what process is it manufactured?
What are its superior features in design and workmanship?
What is its price?
What kind of servicing, if any, will it require?

Answers to these questions about the product being sold are not enough. Similar questions must be answered about competing products. Of particular importance is the question, "What is the major point of difference?" People are inclined to choose an item that affords some advantage not available in a similar item at the same price.

The people to whom sales letters are to be directed. If a sales message is being composed for one certain individual, the more information the writer has about the individual the greater the likelihood of writing an effective letter. If the message is being composed for a certain group, the writer can profitably ask "What characteristics do the members have in common?" "What are their common goals, their occupational levels, their educational status?" Answering such questions assists in seeing problems from the reader's point of view. The empathy thus generated assists in determining what to say and how to say it in such a way that the desired action will be taken.

The specific action wanted. The specific action wanted is *discussed* in the last paragraph, but that action should be *determined* before the first paragraph is begun. After recipients have finished reading, what are they to do? Fill out an order form and enclose a personal check? Return a card requesting a representative to call? Write for more information? If the writer does not make the answers clear, the reader may take no action or take the wrong action.

Some principles of sales-letter composition. The principles of unity, coherence, and emphasis are just as important in sales letters as in other letters. In addition, some other principles are especially helpful in the writing of sales letters:

Concrete nouns and action verbs help the reader to see the product and its benefits more vividly than do abstract nouns and passive verbs.

Specific language is more convincing than general language. General words seem to imply subjectivity unless they are well supported with specifics. Specific language is space consuming (saying something is "great" is less space consuming than saying what makes it so); therefore, sales letters are usually longer than other letters. Yet, sales letters need to be concise; they should say what needs to be said without wasting words.

Reader-centered writing is more effective than product-centered writing. If readers serve as the subjects of sentences, they can visualize themselves with the product in their hands. If they can get the feel of using it for enjoyment or to solve their problems, the chances of creating desire are increased.

A central selling point should permeate the entire letter. Few products are superior by all standards. A thorough product analysis will ordinarily reveal some feature that is different from the features of competing products. This point of difference can be developed into a theme that receives stress throughout. Instead of using a point of difference as a central selling point, a writer may choose to stress one of the major satisfactions derived from using the item. Application of these principles can be seen in examples of letters that follow.

DURING THE WRITING

Only after being thoroughly informed (about the product, competing products, and prospects), and only after preparing an outline should the writing be attempted. The basic outline for persuasive letters presents ideas in the following sequence: getting attention, introducing the product, presenting evidence, and encouraging action. As a writer progresses from one portion of the outline to the next, the following suggestions should prove helpful in the composition.

Getting attention. Various techniques have been successful in getting the recipient to put aside present thoughts or activities and consider the letter:

1. A solution to a problem. "A ball-point pen that writes every time!"
2. A bargain. "Top-quality cigars at $12.45 a hundred!"
3. A proverb. "A penny saved is a penny earned."
4. A news announcement. "INCOME TAXES WILL GO UP 10

PERCENT, the papers are saying. You know what that means for those in our business."

5. An astonishing fact. "Our city spends more for alcohol than for education."
6. A story. "It's 'sale-ring' day at the local stockyards. Let's see what is going on."
7. A quote from a famous person. "We have met the enemy and they are ours," cabled Commodore Perry. We get the same report from those who use our termite killer.
8. An analogy. "Whetstone—the Cadillac of sterling silverware!"
9. A what-if opening. "What if the boss came to your desk and said, 'We're going to increase production by 13 percent' "?
10. An outstanding feature of the product. "Gasoline that will not knock! We have it."
11. An interesting anecdote. "A young sophomore approached his professor's desk and said . . ."
12. A question, "Why does Oriental wool make such good carpets?"
13. A comment on an attached gadget. "Feel the piece of gingham attached to this letter. Notice . . ."
14. A gift. "Accept this silver-plated spoon with our compliments."
15. A fake inside address. For attention-getting purposes, sometimes the first sentence is broken into three or four short lines and placed in the position of the inside address, which is omitted.
16. A split sentence. Some writers have sought to gain attention by placing only the first few words of a sentence on the first line, skipping a line space, and continuing the sentence in what appears to be a second paragraph:

    "You should see . . .

    how easy it is to operate a tractor with
    automatic steering."

Other attention-getting techniques could be added to the preceding list. Regardless of the technique employed, consider the following suggestions:

1. The idea contained in the first sentence (the attention getter) should be related to the product and its virtues. Otherwise, the reader may be confused or resentful.

> Would you like to make a million? We wish we knew how, but we do know how to make you *feel* like a million. Try our mentholated shaving cream.

The sentence seems to suggest that the letter will be about how to make a million, but it is not.

2. The first sentence should introduce (or lead to a quick introduction of) a central selling point. One idea—an outstanding feature of the product or a primary need that it will satisfy—needs to be stressed throughout the entire letter. Since the beginning sentence is in a very emphatic position, it's an ideal sentence for stressing the central selling point.

3. The attention getter should be "you" centered. Since readers are naturally more interested in themselves than in those who write sales letters, "We have just introduced . . ." is not a particularly interesting way to begin.

4. The attention getter should sound interesting. "It has been shown that . . ." may lead a reader to expect a dull discourse.

5. The attention getter should be original. The preceding list of attention-getting devices can be employed without destroying originality. A writer can begin with an anecdote without using one that many others have used previously. Even original ideas may not seem so if they are presented in stereotyped phrases.

6. The first paragraph should be short. The spaces between paragraphs serve three purposes: (1) They show the dividing place between ideas. (2) They improve appearance. (3) They provide convenient resting places for the eyes. A reader is encouraged to take the first step if it's a short one. If possible, let the first paragraph be no longer than three lines, preferably fewer.

Of all possible ways to get attention, perhaps the most dependable is one that makes the reader think "Here is a solution to one of my problems," or "Here is something I can use." We may lead the recipient to this thought by introducing the product in the attention-getting sentence.

Introducing the product. Although the product *can* be introduced in the first sentence, the typical sales letter has an attention-getting sentence that leads to the introduction of the product. Good sales writing does not require that we have separate sentences and paragraphs for each phase of the letter. In writing the sentence that introduces the product, keep the following suggestions in mind.

1. The introduction should be natural. If coherence techniques are being applied well, the second sentence will continue with a thought that was introduced in the first. Notice the abrupt change in thought after the first sentence: "Strained eyes cause bad tempers. The Westview Assn. of Office Managers has been conducting a survey for the last six months. Their primary aim is to improve lighting conditions." Now, in the revision, notice that the second sentence leads smoothly from the first: "Strained eyes cause bad tempers. That's one thing the Westview Assn. of Office Managers learned from their six-month survey. . . ."

2. The introduction should be action centered. Chances for vivid, interesting writing are improved when *people* (instead of products) are used as subjects of sentences. A small amount of product description is only natural; but, for most of the writing, try to place the product in readers' hands and talk about their using it. Notice the contrast: "This 8 mm projector is housed in a die-cast aluminum case. It has a 750-watt projector bulb, a tilt-control knob, and an easy-to-use swing-out film gate." "Lift this projector. See how easy? That's because of the lightweight aluminum case. Now, swing the film gate open and insert the film. All you have to do is keep the film in front . . . See how easily you can turn . . ." In a sense, we don't sell products; we sell what they will do for their users. We sell the pleasure people derive from use. Therefore, time is more profitably spent in writing about *people deriving satisfaction from using a product* than in writing about *the product.*

3. The introduction should stress a central selling point. As observed earlier, a sales letter needs to have a theme—an outstanding feature or a major advantage that competing products do not have. Early introduction of this theme gives it the stress it deserves. For example, if *ease of operation* were the primary feature of a movie projector, the projector would be introduced as an easy-to-operate projector. Throughout, other features would be mentioned; but, from the introduction, this one feature would get more emphasis than the others.

Presenting convincing evidence. Most of the space in a sales letter is devoted to the presentation of evidence. If evidence is lacking, or not presented well, the letter will probably not be successful. In composing these vital paragraphs, keep the following suggestions in mind.

Continue to emphasize the central selling point. A product has a feature that others do not have, or a reader gains an advantage by using this product instead of another—these points need to be kept uppermost in the reader's mind. (Later in this chapter, a sample letter will illustrate the technique.)

Use specific, concrete language. Simply saying a product is "ideal," "efficient," "durable," or "economical" is hardly enough. Without supporting facts, such evaluations are likely to be rejected. Notice the supporting details here: "How can we guarantee NCC carpet to last for 10 years? Because we use Oriental wool exclusively—every fiber is at least 12 inches long. And the longer the raw wool, the greater the strength of the yarns. Count the number of knots per square inch. Our carpets have 400 knots in every square inch. Conventional carpets, which average a life of about five years, have fewer than 100." Presenting such details is more likely to convince a reader than saying "The carpet's great."

Be objective. Superlatives, exaggerations, flowery statements, unsupported claims, incomplete comparisons, and remarks suggesting certainty all run the risk of making letters sound like high-pressure sales talk. One sentence that contains such subjectivity can destroy confidence in an entire letter. An incomplete comparison such as "Our filters make the air cleaner" can turn the reader off. Without revealing the other item of comparison, the statement is meaningless. Cleaner than any other filter, cleaner than one other, cleaner than our last year's model? "The writer is trying to make me think the filter is cleanest of all without taking the responsibility for saying so." If such a thought strikes the reader, the likelihood of accepting a proposal is greatly reduced.

Interpret statements. Instead of merely stating that a refrigerator is frost proof, a letter could profitably continue with some reminders of what the frost-proof feature means to the consumer. Instead of merely presenting dimensions of a radio, a letter could profitably remind the reader that a radio of these dimensions would fit easily into a purse or a shirt pocket.

Give experimental evidence. If research has established that a product is better, a few lines of detail about the research could be very convincing—much more convincing than general remarks that "it has been shown to be superior."

Use enclosures to help convince. Serious consumers like to see supporting facts and figures. When such information is abundant, a writer can place selected points in the letter; and, for those who may need still more information before making up their minds, an enclosure can be included.

Use testimonials and references. One way to convince prospects that they will like a product is to give them concrete evidence that other people like it. The technique should be employed only with the permission of the people involved.

Offer a guarantee or a free trial. When we offer a guarantee or a free trial, we are saying between the lines that we invite scrutiny and comparison; we are willing to have our statements tested.

Talk convincingly about price. Most sales letters should include a mention of price. They should either tell what the price is or say something to assure the reader that the price is not unreasonable. Logically, price should be introduced late in the letter—after most of the advantages have been discussed. For reducing resistance to price, consider the following suggestions:

1. Introduce price only after having presented the product and its virtues.
2. Keep price talk out of the first and last paragraphs—unless price is to be the central selling point (and it seldom is).
3. Mention price in a sentence that relates or summarizes the virtues of the product; that is, in the sentence where price is mentioned, remind the reader of what is being received in return for that price. The virtue is a positive; the money from which the recipient is being asked to part is a negative. Placing the two in the same sentence helps to deemphasize the negative.
4. Employ a complex or compound sentence for stating price.
5. Use figures to illustrate how enough money can be saved to pay for the expenditure.
6. State price in terms of small units. ($12 a month instead of $144 a year)
7. If practical, invite comparison of prices with other products with similar features.
8. If facts and figures are available, use them to illustrate that the price is reasonable.

Regardless of the kind of evidence given, it is given for the purpose of motivating action.

Motivating action. Although the purpose of a persuasive letter is to get action, identifying that action in the *first* paragraph would be hazardous. Only after having presented evidence that a proposal is worthy should a writer state the specific request for action—in the *last* paragraph. For writing the final paragraph, consider the following suggestions:

1. Mention the *specific* action wanted. Just inviting a "response" is not enough. Exactly, what is the reader to do? Return a form? Send a check? Sign and return a card?

2. Allude to the reward for taking action. Readers are more likely to do *what* is wanted if they are at the same time reminded of *why* they should. By alluding to the advantages of taking action, a writer gets a final opportunity to stress the central selling point. It was introduced at the beginning, was talked about throughout the evidence paragraphs, and stopping without a final reference to it would seem like a violation of unity.

3. Present the action as being easy to take. Since people hesitate to do that which is difficult or time consuming, the action should be made as easy to take as possible. Instead of asking for a "letter of response," ask a recipient to check his choice on an enclosed card. The more difficult the action seems, the greater the chances of procrastination or failure to respond at all.

4. Provide a stimulus for quick action. The longer a reader waits to take action, the dimmer our persuasive evidence becomes in the mind. Some commonly used inducements to quick action are *(a)* buy before prices go up, *(b)* buy before the supply is depleted, *(c)* buy before a certain date approaches, *(d)* buy while a bonus is being offered, and *(e)* buy quickly to bet benefits quickly. Sometimes, the attempt to get quick action can do more harm than good, especially if it shouts too loudly for quick action. Because the following expressions are likely to be met with resistance, they should be avoided: Act today. Do it now. Don't delay. Hurry, Hurry, Hurry. Why wait? Don't wait another minute.

5. Ask confidently for action. Little is gained by such statements as "I hope you will . . ." or "If you agree . . ." Between the lines, these expressions convey lack of self-confidence or lack of confidence in the product.

For good appearance, and for emphasis, the last paragraph should be kept fairly short. The preceding suggestions can be incorporated into a paragraph of five or fewer lines, preferably fewer. A subsequent letter will illustrate.

AFTER THE WRITING

Before composing sales letters, writers should identify the ideas to be included and arrange them in proper sequence. They should review some composition principles they intend to employ. During the writing, they should follow the outline and try to apply the principles. After the writing, they should check carefully to see whether improvements can be made. Editing and improving are simplified if the original draft has been typed in double- or triple-spaced form. Asking others for their reactions to the original draft will usually result in improvement.

No point is too small for consideration. Because hundreds or even thousands of copies may be mailed, and because success is measured by the number of responses, the final draft must come as close to perfection as the writer can make it.

A sales letter. To illustrate the application of organizing and writing principles discussed earlier in the chapter, the following letter is discussed sentence by sentence:

> The Gazette delivery boy throws the paper at almost exactly the same time every day.
>
> > *Uses the central point as a device for getting attention and identifying the subject matter.*
>
> And the news stories are just as timely as he is punctual.
>
> > *Employs a sentence closely related to the first.*
>
> For example, you can read up-to-the-minute accounts of important local and national events in less than two hours after they have occurred.
>
> > *Proceeds to give detail to support the idea of timeliness. Uses the reader as the subject of the sentence.*
>
> That's because we keep our news wires open right up to the four-o'clock press time.
>
> > *Continues with additional detail to support the time theme.*
>
> When important news breaks just before press time, our skilled reporters and printers can arrange to include it in *today's* Gazette; you can read it this evening shortly after six o'clock.
>
> > *Gives more support for timeliness. Ties timeliness in with punctual delivery. Employs concrete nouns and action verbs.*
>
> You can read tomorrow's paper at the very same hour.
>
> > *Further emphasizes the central selling point.*
>
> When you can depend on receiving your paper at the same time each day, reading it naturally becomes a habit—a habit that's easy to fit right into your regular routine of family living.

Suggests an advantage of punctual delivery.

Whether you want a first-hand report of Washington affairs, a baseball or football score, or a local wedding, you can have the habit of turning to the Gazette regularly.

Refers to features of the paper in a sentence in which the reader is the subject. "Habit" and "regularly" serve as reminders of the central selling point.

You can turn to the up-to-date Classified Ad section for anything you want to buy, rent, or locate.

Lets the reader take the paper in his hands and use it to solve his problems.

In spite of the inviting front-page stories and the sports, society, and editorial pages, many housewives have told us they look first at the advertising—especially at the grocery sale ads featured daily.

Tells of additional features that make the gazette a good paper to receive daily. "Daily" is a good word choice because it is related to the central selling point.

They say the ads enable them to save many times the $7 monthly subscription rate.

Employs the pronoun "they" as a coherence device. After having presented most of the sales points, introduces price in a sentence that suggests a reward for paying the price. Subordinates price by presenting it in a long paragraph.

For example, this week's Thursday paper will carry a coupon that lets you buy nationally advertised instant coffee for $2.15 (regular $2.49) and frozen TV dinners for $1.49 (regular $1.89). Similar coupons are featured daily.

Gives figures to support the idea of saving money.

You can keep up with the local and national news as a matter of habit.

Uses "habit" as a reminder of the central selling point.

You can take advantage of local advertising as a matter of economy.

Seeks to summarize (as does the sentence before it) the advantages of subscribing.

By subscribing in plenty of time to get Thursday's paper, you save 74 cents on this week's grocery bill.

Follows the summary of advantages immediately with a mention of the action necessary to get them. Shows the reward for quick action.

Please sign and return the enclosed card.

Indicates the specific action desired.

Your delivery boy will then leave the Gazette on your steps around 6:15 each weekday evening. Look at your clock when Thursday's paper comes; from now on you can expect to receive it at almost exactly the same time.

Presents a final reminder of the central selling point.

The preceding letter was written for the purpose of getting someone to buy. The principles of planning and writing are very similar when the letter is written for the purpose of getting someone to take action.

A persuasive claim. Claims letters are often routine; the basis for the claim is a guarantee or some other assurance that an adjustment will be made without need of persuasion. However, when an immediate remedy is doubtful, persuasion is necessary. In the typical large business, the claim letter is passed on to the claims adjuster for response.

In spite of the distasteful aspects of their jobs, claims adjusters are human beings with emotions that can be influenced. Very likely, they have had little or nothing to do with the manufacture and sale of a product; they did not create the need for the claim letter.

In modern businesses, any reasonable claim will probably be adjusted to the customer's satisfaction. Modern businesses appreciate reasonable claims because such claims enable firms to improve their products or services. Therefore, venting strong displeasure in the claims letter is of little value. It can alienate the claims adjuster—the one person from whom cooperation is sought.

From the point of view of the claims adjuster, all claims should receive a fair hearing. Only a small percentage of claims are from "cranks"; the great bulk of claims letters are from people who believe they have a legitimate complaint. The way in which the adjuster handles the claim determines, to a large extent, the goodwill of the company. For the adjuster, granting a claim is much easier than refusing it. Because saying "no" is one of the most difficult writing tasks, the writer of the persuasive claim letter has the advantage of the adjuster.

Notice how the following claim letter presents a sincere statement of the situation and appeals to the business character of the firm. The letter begins with a point on which the reader and writer can agree, presents an adequate description of the reason for the claim, reviews steps needed to remedy the cause, and relies on the letter's basic theme for the closing appeal.

> "Customer satisfaction after the sale," as stated in your advertising, is certainly the cornerstone of your reputation for integrity. It is also the primary reason why you have so much repeat business.
>
> On February 1, just one month ago, I purchased a new "factory-fresh" Cardinal from you, and it functioned well for two weeks. I followed the new car breaking-in instructions to the letter and had little difficulty. But two weeks ago the front wheels developed a frightening vibration that forced me to bring the car to your shop for inspection.
>
> The service manager inspected the wheels, said the bushings had been damaged, and immediately had the old bushings replaced. Later that day, we tested the car together, and it worked satisfactorily. The service manager then asked me to sign the service slip indicating my willingness to pay the repair and parts charges of $98.75. In the discussion that followed, he stated that the bushings could not have been damaged by normal operation but only by careless driving over rough terrain. I refused to pay. He refused to make the bill "no charge." There the matter stood until today, when I received a bill from you for $98.75.
>
> Because I had not driven the car over rough terrain and had taken care of it during the breaking-in period, I can only conclude that the bushings were damaged in the sixty miles the car was driven before I purchased it. Perhaps the damage to the bushings occurred during demonstration trips by salesmen.
>
> Please write "no charge" on the attached bill, proving that your advertising is backed by the integrity you claim.

Knowledge of effective claim writing should never be used as a means of taking advantage of someone. Hiding an unjustifiable claim under a cloak of untrue statements would be very difficult and strictly unethical. Adjusters are fair-minded people who will give the benefit of the doubt, but they are not give-away specialists who would satisfy a grumpy customer simply to avoid a problem. An ethical business follows the Golden Rule.

The letters in this chapter have been directed toward getting a reader to do something—buy a product or accept an idea and act accordingly. The recommended sequence of ideas has been (1) get attention, (2) introduce the idea or product, (3) present evidence, and (4) encourage action. This pattern serves well as a guide; it is not intended as a substitute for imagination and creativity. Writers have abundant opportunity to use their originality when they decide which appeals to use, which words are best, which sentence structure is most appropriate, and so forth.

Like sales letters and persuasive-claim letters, collection letters are written persuasively; but because circumstances surrounding the desired action are different, the persuasive approach is different.

PERSUADING TO PAY

Floods of computerized requests and form and personal letters flow through our mail system daily in an effort to collect money. Business revolves around the use of credit. Credit comes from the Latin word *credere* meaning to believe. The very nature of credit is belief or trust in another person's ability and willingness to uphold an agreement. Credit applicants are evaluated on the basis of the C's of credit—character, capacity, and capital.

Character is the applicant's reputation for meeting monetary obligations: What is the past pay record? Capacity is earning power: Is current income adequate to meet all obligations? And capital is determined by the net worth of an individual: What security exists if earnings decline? Thus, these are sensitive items. To be refused the use of credit indicates a weakness in one or more of the C's. Of course, a fourth C, conditions, could be added to cover those circumstances beyond the control of the individual—the economic health of the community.

The use of credit is an earned privilege, not a given right. Yet, individuals and business firms constantly let obligations go beyond due dates. Fortunately these represent a minority of credit users. Collection tasks are simplified because delinquent debtors have some special characteristics.

Characteristics of the delinquent debtor. First, the delinquent debtor *knows he or she owes.* A bill may have been overlooked inadvertently, but the debtor knows this fact when reminded. Second, those who owe don't mind being asked to pay. Third, because debtors are human, they are subject to emotional or psychological appeal.

Keeping these characteristics in mind, let's see what advantages they give the collection writer. Because the debtor was extended credit on the basis of the C's, he or she has established a reputation as a person who can be trusted. All users of credit are members of a group that underwent some selection. We can assume then that most debtors are honest and would pay if it were possible.

As an emotional person, too, the debtor is susceptible to certain appeals. Gestalt psychology tells us that all people must make closures. That is, when one's world is out of balance, things aren't right until the world is back in balance. A person who owes has an out-of-balance world, and the collection writer takes advantage of this condition by encouraging the delinquent to pay. This task is accomplished through the use of appeals such as:

Fair play: including loyalty, integrity, cooperation.
Pride: including reputation, prestige, accomplishment.
Fear: including loss of possession, privileges, and credit.

Variations of these appeals permit the writer to adapt to almost anyone's ambitions, security, or reputation. And challenges to these human desires elicit emotional responses. The appeals must be honest ones that reveal a degree of faith in the debtor. Threats of physical violence or of damaging action to one's reputation are out of place and could result in legal difficulty for the writer.

In addition to susceptibility to appeals, debtors have other important characteristics based on previous payment practices which classify them as one of the following types of debtors:

Good pay. The debtor whose past practice was always to pay on time.

Good but slow pay. The debtor who always pays but occasionally requires some prodding.

Poor pay. The debtor who was probably granted credit on the chance he or she would change past paying habits—the borderline credit risk.

Good-pay debtors probably need only a simple reminder to induce payment. Strong appeals should be used only as a last resort. Appeals to cooperation and fair play are effective in early collection efforts, and pride and prestige appeals would be effective only after long periods of collection efforts.

The good-but-slow-pay debtor may well be a person of great integrity but be, as well, somewhat disorganized and forgetful, or a procrastinator.

Much like the good-pay debtor, the slow payer may put things off until the creditor shows a degree of impatience.

The poor-pay debtor probably has been down the collection process road before. Straddling the fence between pay and no pay may be a game that isn't decided until legal implications are mentioned. Strong appeals about loss of credit or repossession actions are effective after early reminders prove fruitless. People in this category probably have other shaky credit relationships and will ultimately respond simply because they still have need for credit.

The language of collections. Collection letters, also with letters about credit, have terminology somewhat unusual to business writing. Although not a vocabulary unto itself, the following list of terms represents some language usage important in the credit-collection talk.

Extend. Credit is *extended,* because it is earned. The phrase *grant credit* should not be used, because *grant* implies something for free or in the form of a gift. Therefore, use *extend credit* rather than imply that it wasn't earned.

Delinquent. Although we have used *delinquent* in this discussion to describe one whose payment is past due, the term should not be used in letters to describe people. You may use phrasing to describe an account as delinquent as in "payment is delinquent," but unfavorable implications derive from its use with people. Teenagers are often described as delinquents, and that meaning should be avoided in letters. The following wording is satisfactory: "Your account is past due," and "your payment is delinquent." To be safe, though, avoid the word if possible.

Very, extremely. In difficult collection situations, use adverbs such as *very* and *extremely* to add stringency to writing. A situation may be important, but it takes on power when it is described as "extremely" important. Serious is serious, but a "very serious" problem is acute.

Must, compelled, no other alternative. Use words or phrases like these to add a sense of urgency to messages. "We must have your payment." "You leave us no other alternative."

Mutual, fair, cooperative, agreed, bargain. "We've lived up to our side of the bargain. How about you?" The words listed are effective in pride and fair-play appeals. Although a bit redundant, a combination such as "mutually agreed upon" seems to stress the two-sided nature of credit.

Collection stages. Using knowledge of debtor characteristics, pay habits, and human nature as a basis, collection procedures have become fairly well established within a framework of collection stages. The series of stages incorporates collection messages, which proceed from courteous reminders to strong demands for payment. A maximum would include the following stages:

1. Notice.
2. Reminder.
3. Inquiry.
4. Appeal.
5. Strong appeal or urgency.
6. Ultimatum.

Notice and reminder stages most often are handled by duplicate copies of billings containing statements such as "past due" or "please remit." All but serious delinquencies are usually cleared at these stages. Tone of collection efforts must be courteous and show concern for goodwill by appearing to be routine. The collection writer's assumption at the notice and reminder stages is that payment was simply overlooked.

The inquiry stage occurs after the normal number of reminders have been sent without success. The assumption here is that nonpayment is symptomatic of something wrong. Collection efforts try to get some action from the debtor by using a helpful tone. The gist of inquiry is to offer help if something is wrong and, if nothing is wrong, to receive payment. Here is a typical inquiry letter taken from a form collection series used by a personal finance company.

> Dear Friend
>
> The payment on your travel loan is twenty days overdue and another payment will soon be due. If there is some reason why you are unable to make this payment, will you let me know by telephoning or by writing an explanation on the back of this letter and returning it in the enclosed return envelope.
>
> Otherwise, may we have your check right away.
>
> Cordially

For those debtors who haven't responded to the inquiry, the collection writer must use persuasion to elicit payment. This is done by selecting the most appropriate appeal for the individual case. The appeal letter deals with the sensitive C characteristics—character, capital, capacity. Probably the weakest appeal is one that says "If you don't pay us, we can't pay our bills." That puts both the debtor and the creditor in the poor-pay category. Good appeal letters (1) review the situation, (2) develop a single appeal, (3) describe the necessary action for the debtor to take, and (4) request action. Notice how the following letter appeals to fair play:

Dear Mr. Smith

Ten weeks ago we shipped 12 dozen Whoozits to you as the first purchase charged to your new account.

The mutual contract we entered into was based on two things—our ability to make delivery as agreed and your ability to pay as agreed, an ability, incidentally, that was apparent in comments we received from your credit references. You'll have to agree that we kept our part of the bargain. The only way to complete the agreement is for you to do your part by sending your check for $316 today.

Please slip the check in the enclosed envelope now—while this letter is before you.

Cordially

The strong appeal letter normally follows the appeal letter and attempts to stress the urgency of the situation. "We must have the payment . . ." is the general tone of the strong appeal. Frequently, "for your own good" stresses the nature of a self-preservation appeal. At any rate, the letter used at this stage tries to obtain payment through every effort short of issuing an ultimatum or last-chance letter. A usual practice is to have these letters signed by a senior executive to impress on the debtor the seriousness of the problem. Notice how the following letter uses a fear appeal to develop urgency.

Dear Mr. Smith

As you well know, the use of credit is an earned privilege—earned on the basis of the applicant's character, capacity, and capital. The routine check we made before extending credit to you revealed you met these three requirements.

I was disappointed when your account was referred to me. Because legal action is always costly, accounts reaching the critical condition yours is in come to me before being turned over to our legal department.

Won't you, for both our benefits, return your check in the enclosed envelope, which will come directly to me. I must hear from you within five days.

Sincerely

Often, at the urgency stage, the technique of giving the debtor a choice between two or more methods of solving the problem, such as sending payment or signing an interest-bearing note. In any case, urgency letters let the debtor know very clearly that collection will ultimately be made.

At the ultimatum stage, the letter simply indicates that if payment is not received within a certain time, legal action will commence. An ultimatum is the final letter, and the tone is "now or never."

Form collection series. The following principles establish the framework for firms planning to use form collection letter series:

1. Collection problems must be frequent, and thus, routine.
2. Collection problems must be of the same nature.
3. Secured loans lend themselves most readily to form collection letters.

One oil company uses over 200 form collection letters. All are computerized and are issued based on three criteria: The length of time the customer has had a credit card, the period amounts are past due, and the amount past due. For example, a customer having a 30-day past-due amount in excess of $50 dollars and having had a card for less than a year would get a letter specially written for that situation. If the amount reaches 45 days past due, a different letter would be issued.

Except for the most routine early stages, even form letters should be individually typed so they can be personalized with names, amounts, and dates. One rule holds true: If the letter is an obvious form, don't try to camouflage it. The debtor recognizes a mimeographed or auto-typed letter as a form, particularly when fillers are inserted by a different typewriter.

Other collection problems. In addition to the usual collection series, other letters must be written for unusual cases. For example, the debtor who always pays 20 days late may simply have a pay day that falls at any inconvenient time. Here's an example of such a letter:

Dear Mr. Blank

Thank you for your March 1 payment which was received yesterday, March 20.

Although we are pleased with the regularity of your payments, we do wonder if a different due date would be more convenient. Your payments generally are received around the twentieth of each month.

If a change of date would assist you, make a note at the bottom of this letter and return it to me. Otherwise, we ask that you make payments on the first as scheduled.

Sincerely

The problem of collecting unearned discounts plagues many manufacturers and wholesalers. A bill providing a discount for prompt payment is often ignored until well after the discount date and then paid with the discount deducted. In these cases, a simple notation on the next bill calls attention to the problem:

The additional amount on your bill represents the discount you may have taken inadvertently when you paid your last bill after the discount period.

Of course, persistent deductions of the discount by a party calls for the use of regular collection procedures.

Using the telephone and telegram in collections. For local problems, the telephone provides a quick and inexpensive collection tool. Notices, reminders, and inquiries can all be handled by phone. In a sense, the telephone call does three jobs at once: (1) It completes early collection stages quickly. (2) It provides for instant feedback by the debtor. (3) Because of the two-way communication, it enables the creditor to maintain goodwill. When the telephone is used in long-distance collecting, it creates a sense of urgency. Therefore, long-distance collecting by phone should be reserved for urgency cases. Those who collect by telephone should become familiar with state laws. Calling too frequently or during normal sleeping hours is inadvisable and probably illegal.

Like long-distance telephone calls, telegrams add a sense of urgency and should be reserved for later stages in collections. Day-letter and night-letter telegrams may delay delivery for a few hours compared to full-rate telegrams. On the other hand, they are less expensive and can include up to fifty words for the basic rate. In either case, telegrams, like registered letters, provide the creditor with evidence that the message was received. From this viewpoint alone, they are valuable in difficult collection cases.

Why study collections? Because credit is a rather cherished institution, the problem of collecting past-due amounts of money deals with a sensitive area of human behavior. Writing effective collection messages while still maintaining a degree of goodwill is a most valuable art and skill. The carry-over values into other writing tasks is considerable.

Summary. Before writing an action-seeking letter, a writer should first try to determine whether the action would be taken willingly or whether it would be taken only after persuasion. If persuasion is thought necessary, the inductive approach is recommended.

Through inductive writing, readers are given an *incentive* before being asked to *act.* Typical action-seeking letters are designed to sell ideas or products, get special favors, or collect money. The recommended outline for such letters: get attention, introduce a product or idea, give evidence, and encourage action.

Success in sales writing can hardly be expected if careful planning has not preceded. Before writing, the following considerations should be taken into account: the product and how it differs, the people to whom the letters are directed, and the specific action wanted. Concrete nouns, action verbs, and specific language are especially helpful in sales writing. Effective sales writing is reader centered; it also stresses one central idea that permeates the entire letter.

Like sales letters, persuasive claim letters draw attention to a problem, present arguments, and *then* ask for favorable action. Although one who writes a claim letter may feel angry or disappointed, sarcasm or abusive language should be avoided. That principle applies also to collection writing.

Typically, collection letters are shorter than other persuasive letters. Debtors usually know already that they owe. A fairly short letter that presents one point emphatically is superior to a long letter that presents many points (each of which competes with others for attention). In collection letters, typical appeals (incentives for paying) are fair play, pride, and fear. The collection process moves through various stages: notice, reminder, inquiry, appeal, urgency, and ultimatum. If collection is unsuccessful at one stage, a writer moves to the next stage. Except for the appeals stage (which may include several letters), one letter is written at each stage. The final stage (the ultimatum) reveals the action the writer will take if payment is not received.

In all persuasive writing, one principle is paramount: before asking for action, let the reader see why action is beneficial or justified.

Chapter 9

WRITING SPECIAL LETTERS

A variety of special situations occurs so regularly that the good writer should have no problems with them. Most, too, have to do with personal relationships and sensitive problems.

CONDOLENCE OF SYMPATHY

From an etiquette point of view, the letter of sympathy to the family of a friend who has died must be written promptly. Yet, this is a most difficult writing problem. One way to handle it, although a little impersonal, is to send a card with the handwritten message "Deepest Sympathy." Telegrams may be used with messages such as "Deeply saddened by your loss. Sympathy to you and your family." When written, the message should be handwritten, although usage now permits typed messages when the deceased is a business associate. The simplest plan is to start with a statement of sympathy, follow with a sentence conveying your interest, close with some words of comfort and affection. For a letter to the widow of a deceased acquaintance for example:

> Dear Mrs. Smith
>
> I was deeply sorry to hear of your sad news. Jim was a genuinely fine person with whom I spent many enjoyable and satisfying times. He will be greatly missed by those of us who worked with him in the

Chamber of Commerce. Please accept my warmest sympathy and best wishes.

Most sincerely

Also, when a close relative such as spouse, son, daughter, mother, or father of a close friend dies, you should write the friend a letter of sympathy.

CONGRATULATIONS

All too often we read of the promotion, election, or other significant achievement by an acquaintance and think how nice it would be to congratulate the person only to forget it promptly. In terms of building good will for yourself and your organization, take the time to send a short note. It will be appreciated—and might even be the only note the other person receives, thus making your thoughtfulness really stand out.

Some executives accomplish this good will gesture by using one of a supply of note cards which is always available. A handwritten message is satisfactory, and a typed one enables you to say more. Births, weddings, and engagements are other circumstances calling for congratulatory messages, particularly when those involved are employees of your firm.

Here's a short letter of congratulations on the occasion of a promotion:

Dear Jim

I just read of your election to President and Chief Executive Officer. Please accept my warmest congratulations and best wishes for every future success.

Sincerely

Both letters of condolence and congratulations should be acknowledged. Acknowledgment of a letter of condolence could be as simple as "Thank you for your kind expression of sympathy," and it should be handwritten. For a letter of congratulations, a typed business reply might take the following form:

Dear George

Thanks so much for your nice words about my promotion and for the good wishes. I look forward to continuing to work with you. It's always a pleasure.

Sincerely

RECOMMENDATIONS

Letters of recommendation about employees or friends take two forms. One is the solicited recommendation requested by a business organization, and the other is the unsolicited letter which is requested by the individual to incorporate in an employment dossier. The first will be addressed to a specific person or organization; the second may be headed by "To Prospective Employers." Generally, the solicited letter will reply to specific concerns of the prospective employer as outlined in a request. The unsolicited letter will be broader in nature and contain statements about work performance, attitude, and potential.

If the one written about can be endorsed with enthusiasm, the letter should be written deductively. If the endorsement cannot be strong, an inductive plan permits the use of negatives, but subordinates them. A device used by good writers to de-emphasize mild comments and stress favorable ones is to place the name of the person talked about in the independent part of a complex sentence and the pronoun in the dependent part. Note the difference in the following pair of sentences:

1. Although *John* is only a fair golfer, *his* amiability and integrity should make him a good club member.
2. Although *he* is only a fair golfer, *John's* amiability and integrity should make him a good club member.

Because readers gain greater communication from the independent part of a sentence, the second version of the sentence, which is an independent clause, not only stresses John's strengths but uses his name as well. People pay more attention to proper nouns than to pronouns.

In the following letter recommending a person for club membership, notice how the writer has endorsed the candidate enthusiastically while using the preceding illustration to subordinate his golfing ability:

Gentlemen

As a member of Lakefront Country Club for over twenty years, I endorse without reservation the nomination of Charles R. Jones for membership.

Charles has been active in community affairs, has a fine family of five, and is well known in legal and business circles because of his successful law practice. Although he is only a fair golfer, Charles' amiability and integrity should make him a good club member.

I would be pleased to represent him at the membership interview if desired.

Sincerely

INTRODUCTIONS

Social and business courtesy contribute to the practice of providing letters of introduction for others. In such a letter, introduce the person, give a reason for the introduction, mention something about the person's background, and thank the reader. Letters of introduction should, of course, be sent only to close acquaintances. Here's an example:

Dear Steve

I hope you can take a few minutes of your time to talk with Roger Jones, who will be visiting in San Francisco next week.

Roger is the new U.S. representative for Cuttydunn, Ltd., and is making his first visit to the West Coast. Prior to this appointment, he was in charge of their European operations.

I've asked him to call your office for an appointment and will appreciate any courtesy you can show him.

Cordially

RESERVATIONS

The letter of reservation for hotel accommodations should be very specific in terms of arrival time, days to stay, type of room, and confirmation. For example:

Gentlemen

Please reserve a single room for me for the nights of June 11, 12, and 13. I shall arrive about 6 p.m. on June 11 and depart at noon on June 14.

I shall appreciate a prompt confirmation.

Very truly yours

INVITATIONS

The informal invitation resembles a business letter. It is desirable to use smaller paper than regular business letterhead. Your wording should be conversational, as though you were making the invitation orally. As a matter of style, the inside address should be placed following the letter:

Dear Mr. and Mrs. Smith

You are cordially invited to attend the annual Installation Ball of the Chamber of Commerce at the Surfrider Hotel on January 10. Cocktails will be served at 6:30 p.m. followed by dinner and dancing. Please RSVP to my office at 777-4183 by January 4. I hope to see you there.

Cordially

Mr. and Mrs. Theodore Smith
444 Commonwealth
Beverly Hills, California

The invitation should be acknowledged promptly. When a telephone RSVP is not mentioned, either a typed or handwritten reply is satisfactory and should use the same conversational style as the invitation used.

Formal invitations are generally printed, and a printer can provide examples. At the same time, however, many formal invitations are handwritten, especially for smaller groups. When the affair is to be black tie, the invitation should include that notation. Here is an example of a formal invitation:

Mr. and Mrs. George L. Dawes
request the company of
Mr. and Mrs. Robert B. Clarkon
at dinner
on Saturday, the twelfth of June
at seven-thirty o'clock
635 South Maryland Avenue
Chicago, Illinois

Black Tie

A reply to such an invitation should be written in longhand and follow, as much as possible, the same style. Wording such as the following is appropriate: Mr. and Mrs. Robert B. Clarkon accept with pleasure the invitation of Mr. and Mrs. George L. Dawes for dinner on Saturday, the twelfth of June at seven thirty o'clock.

RESIGNATIONS

When an employee leaves one firm to accept employment in another, employers normally expect a written statement of resignation. Tone and length are determined by circumstances surrounding the resignation. An employee who is leaving under rather unpleasant circumstances would probably include no more than (1) the job title, (2) the resignation, and (3) the effective date:

> I resign my position as administrative assistant in the accounting department. My last day of service will be June 30, 1981.

If the urge to take a final stab at a superior, a colleague, or the firm cannot be resisted, include it; but hold the letter for a day or two and read it over. By then, the wisdom of its deletion will almost certainly be evident.

The resignation letter may also include information about the position or firm into which the employee is moving, a limited amount of reminiscence, and an expression of gratitude:

> I resign my position as administrative assistant in the accounting department.
>
> From my very first day in the department, I have appreciated the friendly atmosphere, the efficient teamwork, and the encouragement to grow professionally.

After receiving my accounting degree on June 15, I will be moving to San Francisco and beginning my career as an auditor on July 15.

My experience here at ATWELL has been very gratifying.

My last day of service will be June 30, 1981.

Sincerely

SUMMARY

Special letters have to do with personal relationships and sensitive problems. Such letters are short, seldom longer than just a few lines.

Condolence letters should be sent promptly. Sympathy may be expressed by writing "Deepest Sympathy" at the bottom of a printed card. Or a short letter may be handwritten (typewritten if the deceased is an associate). The letter normally includes a statement of sympathy, a sentence conveying interest, and some words of comfort or affection.

Congratulatory letters may be either handwritten or typewritten. Because the letters are about something positive, the letters are easy to write. Because so many people don't bother to write or simply procrastinate until too much time has passed, the letters that *are* received make positive and lasting impressions.

In recommendation letters, fairness is paramount—fairness to the job applicant as well as to future employers. Most applicants invite recommendations only from people who can report positives; thus, recommendations are relatively easy to write. When negatives are reported, they are best subordinated.

Introductions, reservations, invitations, and resignations (like other special letters) are short, factual, and courteous.

Chapter 10

PREPARING PERSONAL RÉSUMÉS

Sending a written message is not the only approach to getting a job. In some instances, it may not even be the best approach. But it's a good one—a good one if the applicant (1) is a person who deserves a job, (2) locates a job possibility, (3) analyzes the job and the preparation for it, (4) prepares an effective job résumé, and (5) writes an appropriate letter.

BE A PERSON WHO DESERVES A JOB

Only those who deserve a job should write for one. They should be able to give affirmative answers to the following questions:

1. Do I want to work? A commendable attitude is "I want to do something worthwhile and for that service I wish to receive a reasonable reward."

2. Can I do something specific? If an employer has a job open, he wants someone who can do the specific tasks for which the job calls. He is not likely to be impressed with the young applicant who wants any job that is open. Those who are prepared for a specific job have an advantage. Since businesses appreciate personnel who make and take advantage of opportunities in business life, they are impressed with young people who have obviously planned their personal lives.

3. Would I be loyal? In a sense, all employees are ambassadors for their firms. In return for their salaries, they are expected to do good work, but more, too. They are members of a team. Their jobs depend on the firm's success. Therefore, they conduct themselves in such a way as to reflect honor on their firms. To those outside the firm, they speak of it in a favorable light. They explain its actions and interpret its goals if necessary. If interviewees cast aspersions on their present employers, the interviewer's reaction is likely to be nega-

tive: "Avoid this applicant. If hired, the applicant would seen be knocking the new employer."

4. Would I be co-operative? Business wants people with ideas of their own, but it also wants workers who have consideration for the ideas of others.

5. Do I have initiative? Employers need workers who have initiative. Those with enough initiative to prepare a job résumé and write a letter of application may demonstrate initiative in their work.

LOCATE A JOB POSSIBILITY

One who has products to sell develops a list of prospects. One who has service to sell should develop a list of job possibilities. The following sources of information are particularly helpful:

Libraries. If some of the following sources fail to provide the job leads in which you are interested, ask your librarian for help:

Annual reports from major firms
Career, the *Annual Guide to Business Opportunities*
Company house organs
Dictionary of Occupational Titles
Engineering Index
Fortune
Industrial Arts Index
Moody's *Manuals*
Occupational Outlook Handbook
Readers' Guide
Science Research Associates' occupational information pamphlets
Standard and Poor's *Manuals*
Trade and professional journals
U.S. News and World Report
Wall Street Journal

Newspaper ads. Promptness is sometimes the key factor in answers to newspaper ads. If you use newspapers as a medium, get your letter and résumé in the mail as quickly as possible after the edition comes off the press. The first letters received may be considered more carefully than the last ones. And the trait of promptness is a personal virtue that your prospective employer will regard as a business virtue.

Have the application and résumé ready. Then, you can easily and quickly adapt them to the job for which you apply.

Newspaper and magazine articles. If an article tells about the laying of a cornerstone for a new bank or the planned-for expansion of a manufacturing facility, that means new employees will probably be needed. If marketing forecasts precict booms in home building, you may expect to find new job openings in real estate, escrow, insurance, or lending institutions.

Letters of inquiry. One way to learn whether jobs are available in your area of interest is to write and ask. Any firm needing workers in your category will very likely send you an application form.

Professional organizations. Job seekers who are applying for professional jobs should be familiar with associations within their profession. Some such journals have help-wanted and positions-wanted columns. Sometimes, the officers of professional organizations gather and disseminate job information.

Company representatives. Representatives of insurance firms, book publishers, office-machine distributors, and so forth, are sometimes glad to share their information about job opportunities.

Teachers. Especially while still in school, students can get some job information from teachers. Many businessmen have come to depend on schools as their source of employees, and they let teachers know when they need new employees.

School placement bureaus. Although placement officials may not be able to hunt actively for a job you can fill, they can be very helpful by (1) serving as a repository for your credentials, (2) compiling information about job opportunities, and (3) arranging for interviews. Many firms send company representatives to college campuses regularly for recruitment purposes.

Telephone. A personnel office with a recruitment problem appreciates your calling to ask whether applications are wanted.

Public and private employment agencies. For public agencies, there is no charge; but, of course, the private agency will have to extract a fee if you accept a job it recommends. Because the fee is based on the first month's salary, the private agency has incentive to find you a high paying job.

Walk-ins. Some firms depend on walk-ins as their major source of workers. By walking in and inquiring, you might get a short interview or an application form, thus making writing unnecessary and saving time.

Friends and relatives. Some firms encourage their employees to recommend prospective workers. Others, however, may want to avoid the possibility of cliques among their workers; they are not inclined to honor suggestions made by employees or relatives. If a relative provides a job lead, ask whether the firm has a policy on nepotism. Some firms have a definite policy against the hiring of relatives.

ANALYZE THE JOB AND YOUR PREPARATION FOR IT

The main purpose of a job résumé and an application letter is to get an interview. Afterward, they may be scrutinized again to see if the interview corroborated the first impression. Ordinarily, the résumé and application letter are considered successful if they get an interview; but a candidate who is given an interview but later loses out when they are compared with other letters and résumés has not necessarily written a successful letter. The most successful letters lead the prospective employer to think, "I believe this applicant can do what we want done." If you are to lead the employer to this conclusion, you must have a clear idea of (1) what the job entails and (2) your preparation for doing it. And, of course, you have to write convincingly; you have to show how the preparation matches the job.

Before you convince the employer, you have to convince yourself. On one side of a sheet, write down everything you know about the job. You have a chance to learn about the job through several media: (1) Your occupational courses in school. If, for example, you are applying for a junior accountant's job, you should have a good idea of what tasks a junior accountant performs. Or, if you are applying for placement in a management-trainee program, your management courses should be helpful in a general way. (2) The *Dictionary of Occupational Titles.* Although job titles do not always give accurate descriptions of the work performed by someone who has that title in a specific firm, they do give you a general idea. (3) A visit to a branch office, if that is convenient. (4) A talk with former employees. (5) A talk with workers who perform a similar job for another company. (6) The firm's annual report or any other information that you can get from its employment office. And while you are learning about the specific job you want, learn as much as possible about the company. If you can learn who your supervisor would be and what that person's viewpoints are, do so. The more information you have, the better are your chances for making a sound decision.

These instructions may seem elementary. Yet it's one thing to *know* something should be done but another to *do* it. A college-campus recruiter for one of the largest firms in the country had some lamentations at the end of a long day of interviewing. He said it was obvious that not a single applicant had done any research on his company before the interview. In fact, most of them had not even read the pamphlets given to them by the school placement bureau when they had made the interview appointment. According to the interviewer, the candidates were "not hungry enough." His firm was not interested in prospective employees who showed such an astonishing lack of interest or initiative. The more you know about your prospective employer, the easier it will be for you to write to and talk with him or her.

Now that you have filled up one side of a page with information about the requirements of the job, fill up the other side with information about yourself. The common tendency is to say, "I can digest all this job- and self-analysis information and just keep it in my mind. No need to bother writing it down." But remember, the employer is going to get an impression from the written facts. Put them down and see how you would react. If your self-analysis reveals a startling lack of preparation, begin making plans to get it or seek a different job. Good writing, of course, is helpful; but you can never count on it as a substitute for the training, experience, and education necessary for the job you want. Opposite the training required for the job, list the training you have had. Do the same for experience, education, and other factors. Ask yourself whether the job would lead to your life's goals. Do some serious thinking about your strengths and weaknesses.

Keep those job- and self-analysis notes; they will help you prepare a job résumé.

PREPARE A RÉSUMÉ

Times have changed the style of application letters. No longer do we attempt to compose a long letter that includes all pertinent data. Nowadays, personnel managers prefer to receive application letters accompanied with a sheet of factual information.

The résumé goes by various names—personal data sheet, summary, qualification sheet, or personal profile. Ordinarily, it is clipped to the back of the application letter. Therefore, the personnel office reads it after having read the application letter. But the résumé should be written first. Preparing it first forces the applicant to do some job- and self-evaluation before writing. Preliminary thinking and evaluation are good mental preparation for writing the letter.

The résumé and the letter of application serve different purposes. One does not repeat the other. The résumé *summarizes all pertinent information* about the applicant. The letter *interprets the information.* Typically, applicants examine their résumés and select the most outstanding facts. Then, in their letters, they point out how by these facts they are qualified to do what the employer wants done. The résumé is usually treated like any other enclosure—alluded to in the last few lines of the letter.

The résumé saves both time and effort for reader and writer. If readers are primarily interested in an applicant's work experience, they can locate it quickly on the data sheet; it is listed under an obvious heading. And they can get the facts quickly because they are in summary form. At first thought, a writer may think it takes more effort to prepare both a letter and a data sheet than to write a lengthy letter. For those who are not accustomed to typing, the tabulation required on a data sheet may appear to be somewhat of a problem. But this problem is offset by the ease of composition. For example, an applicant who chooses not to include a résumé may stop to ponder the various ways of expressing age: "I am 21 years old," "I have just passed my 21st birthday," "My age is 21 years," or "I'll be 22 on my next birthday." On the résumé, its' simple: "Age, 21."

By arranging their résumés in a pleasing manner and presenting data in appropriate sequence, job seekers give proof of their ability to organize. Various formats are acceptable. A résumé makes a good impression if the typing is done so that space is used economically without giving a crowded appearance and if the headings are obvious enough to make finding them easy. If you need a guide, you can always find sample arrangements in a typing text or a secretary's handbook. The models on page 85 (Figure 10–1) are acceptable; so are others.

Most of the information included on a data sheet can be divided into the following categories: (1) Experience, (2) Education, (3) Personal details, and (4) References. If you want to be conventional, begin with the personal details and end with references. If you want to be more modern (and more practical), begin with the category you wish to emphasize most. The first position is most emphatic. If you have had little experience but have just finished college, your most distinctive selling point is probably your education.

If education is to be emphasized more than experience, let education occupy the first section of the résumé sheet. Since the employer will be less interested in personal details than in education and experience, place personal details in a subordinate position. Just before references would be a good place. The last section of the sheet is a good place for references. Now that the employer has read your letter and the foregoing parts of the résumé, it's just natural for you to end by inviting inquiries of others for more information.

If you have accumulated considerable experience, you may conclude that your most outstanding qualification for a new job is not education but experience. Then, emphasize experience by placing it in first position. Should you tell all your experience, part-time and full-time? Yes, for those who have had little experience; no, for those who have had a great variety.

If you are just getting out of school, you may never have held a full-time job. If not, perhaps you worked for short periods between school terms. Rare indeed is the young person who has had no experience at all. And rare, too, is the graduate who would want to advertise lack of experience by listing on the résumé, "Experience: None." If job seekers have actually had no work experience, they may be able to mention fraternities, clubs, or other groups in which they have held positions of responsibility. They would want to make a definite selling point of education. Instead of using the negative sounding "no experience," they could list the specialized training courses that have prepared them for entry into the occupation.

But almost all who have done a good job of self- and job-analysis will see how some of their experiences have been good preparation for the job they want. A part-time filling station attendant who is being graduated and looking for his first accounting job can still list something under the heading "Experience." True, he can't call it "accounting experience"; but it's "work experience" and pretty good experience, too. He can profitably analyze the ways in which his filling station work and accounting work are similar. Most station attendants have some records to keep and most accountants have to handle money. Both have to be accurate. Both may have keys to the premises. Both need to be punctual. Both have some contact with the public. Both have to work long hours in certain seasons. The conduct of either to a certain extent determines the profits of the business. If management had no faith in an attendant's ability to accept responsibility, the attendant would no longer have a job. The same is true of an accountant. Furthermore, people tend to judge our capacity to perform one job by our performance on another. Even if accounting and filling station work were less related, management would still be inclined to believe that a part-time station attendant with a record of dependability would also be a dependable accountant.

By the same token, a student who served as a janitor or a cook while in college does have some work experience to report. These facts should be reported on the résumé and interpreted in the letter of application. The fact that a student has worked at any part-time job while in school is a recommendation in itself. Even though the work may have provided little valuable experience, it does suggest that the candidate has some initiative. It somehow suggests that education was considered important enough to work for it. And those who really want an education are inclined to apply themselves on the job.

Naturally, those who have a variety of work experiences have an advantage. They can choose the experiences most related to the job for which they are applying. No rule says you have to report your experiences in chronological order. Why not list first the experience that is most related and end with the one that ranks next in order of relatedness? In this way, you gain emphasis on the experiences that deserve it.

No rule says you have to list *every* job you ever held. To do so might result in a list so long that your outstanding experiences are de-emphasized. Also, a long list may suggest that you have moved about too much. It may suggest that you were unpopular on your jobs or that you were occupationally unsettled. In either case, the reaction is negative. Of course, if you are filling out an application form, give the information in the order called for in the form. If you are making your own data sheet (résumé), however, you are free to list the most relevant experience and then indicate that you have at times held other jobs.

Try to apply the following guides in preparing your résumé: (1) Choose the format most suitable for you; make the arrangement neat and uncrowded. (2) Arrange the categories of information in the best psychological sequence. (3) Use phrases rather than complete sentences wherever practical; this procedure will save space and make for parallel construction. (4) Put all the information on one page if you can; thus, you will list only important facts and save time for the personnel department. But there is no rule against using two or more pages if necessary. (5) Keep the résumé factual; your letter is the persuasive instrument that interprets the facts.

Look at the résumé illustrated in Figure 10–1.

The *title* identifies the sheet as a résumé for a certain person; it also reveals the nature of the work being sought. The title is such that copies of the sheet could be sent to many different firms. The sheet could be made to appear tailor-made for a specific firm by changing the title to "Charles B. Hay's Résumé: A Career in Finance and Management with XYZ Company." In the mind of an XYZ official, an applicant who makes the effort to adapt the résumé to the company may have some desirable qualities not possessed by competing applicants.

The *education* section appears first because the applicant considers his education a greater asset than experience. As years go by and experience accumulates, experience will deserve first place position on the résumé. Only the most closely related courses are listed. Listing all courses would require too much space and take emphasis away from the most pertinent courses. The grade average is interpreted because not all schools use a 4-point system in computing averages. If education had not extended beyond the bachelor's degree, the applicant would probably have listed the high school from which he was graduated. To stress the fact that education was directly related to the job sought, the applicant could have changed the section title from "Education" to "Education in Finance and Management."

The *experience*, likewise, could have been titled "Job-Related Experiences" or "Related Experiences in Finance and Management" to indicate a closeness of relationship between previous jobs and the job sought. Because the applicant considered the experience as a graduate assistant to be of greater importance than the other experiences, it was listed first. The parenthetical statements about duties performed are especially helpful to a reader who is trying hard to see how past experiences have prepared an applicant for the job sought.

The *other responsibilities* section seems appropriate for this applicant, but it need not be included in all résumés. It does provide some clues

FIGURE 10–1

CHARLES B. HAY'S RÉSUMÉ: A CAREER IN FINANCE AND MANAGEMENT

Education

Master of Business Administration Degree, University of Michigan, August, 1981.
Among the Business and Economics courses taken:

Managerial Finance	Research and Report Writing
Managerial Accounting	Marketing Concepts
Managerial Economics	Business Policy

Grade average: 3.45 (on a scale in which 4 is an A; 3, B; 2, C; 1, D)

Bachelor of Science in Financial Administration, Kansas State University, 1979.
Among the Business and Economics courses taken:

Principles of Management	Business Law	Tax Accounting
Principles of Finance	Business Communication	Human Relations
Financial Institutions	Managerial Decisions	Public Relations

Grade average: 3.65

Experience

Graduate Assistant, University of Michigan, 1980-81. (Assisted Dr. John Snell in preparing, proctoring, and grading tests. Evaluated term reports.)

Part-time Teller, First National Bank, Manhattan, Kansas, 1978-79. (Worked two hours daily at the Drive-up Window.)

Part-time Cashier, Wilson's Discount Stores, Manhattan, Kansas, 1977-78. (Took inventories and stocked shelves, in addition to operating the cash register.)

Other Responsibilities

As a graduate student:
Vice president, MBA club
Intern fellowship, Mutual Life Insurance Association

As an undergraduate student:
Treasurer, Alpha Kappa Psi
Secretary, Senior Class
Senator, College of Business

As a high school student:
Member, National Honor Society
Representative to Boys' State

As a community servant:
Tennis instructor, Parks and Recreation Dept.

Personal Information

Birth date: September 25, 1958. Marital status: Single. Height: 5'11"
Recreational interests: Playing tennis, watching football and baseball
Address (until August 31, 1981): 1401 Bolt Street, Ann Arbor, Michigan 48106
Telephone: 517 926-5622

References (by permission)

Dr. John Snell
Professor of Finance
University of Michigan
Ann Arbor, Michigan 48104

Mr. John White
Branch Manager
First National Bank
114 West Boulevard
Manhattan, Kansas 66502

Mr. Harry W. Wilson
President, Wilson Stores
441 West Fourth Street
Manhattan, Kansas 66502

FIGURE 10–2

MARTHA R. COBB

Qualifications for the position of
Training Director
Western Savings and Loan Association

2162 Seventh Street Indio, California 91101 714-938-4225

Training-Oriented Experiences

Training Director, Bank of the Southwest, Indio, California, 1978 to present. In my current position, I am responsible for designing and implementing short- and long-term training programs for over 250 employees of an eight-branch banking organization. Programs range from new-employee orientation and teller training to middle-management leadership training. Over thirty programs have been or are being offered, and I have personally instructed in some of them.

Assistant Dean, College of Continuing Education, Denver University (Colorado), 1974-78. As Assistant Dean, I was responsible for initiating and planning job-oriented and cultural programs for the Denver community. This work included designing training syllabi based on job requirements surveys, planning schedules, budgeting, and coordinating instructional efforts.

Laboratory and Training Assistant, Department of Instructional Technology, Denver University, 1972-74. My duties in instructional technology were to supervise preparation of audio and visual teaching aids and to operate and maintain technical equipment including video recorders and play-back devices.

Relevant Positions

Teller and New Accounts Representative, Ajax Savings and Loan, Denver, part- and full-time employee, 1968-74.

Instructor, Marvel Health Studios, Arvada, Colorado, 1967-68.

Education

M.S. in Education, Major in instructional technology, Denver University, 1974.

B.S. in Business Administration, Major in organizational behavior and communication, Colorado State University, 1967.

Affiliations

American Society of Training Directors, American Management Association, Beta Gamma Sigma, Phi Delta Kappa, Pi Beta Phi Sorority (President, 1966), National Education Association.

A Personal View

Birth Date: March 26, 1945 5'6" and 120 pounds
Divorced, one daughter Perfect health

Interests include physical fitness, hiking, bridge, public speaking, and reading.

References will be furnished on request.

about the applicant's ability to learn, willingness to accept responsibility, ability to get along with others, and desire to be of service.

The *personal information* requires less space than any other section. It is further subordinated by its position on the sheet. Other personal details could have been included, but the interview would probably be a better place for revealing them. If the address *after* August 31 were known, it could have been included.

The *references* section presents names, titles, and addresses as they would appear on a letter or envelope. Note that each name is preceded by a courtesy title and followed by the official title. Since education was the applicant's strongest asset, at least one of the references had to be from the educational field. Some applicants prefer not to include a list of references for fear that knowledge of job seeking efforts will result in human-relations problems on the present job. Those who think it best not to include references usually indicate that a list of references will be provided on request or at the interview.

Now compare the résumé in Figure 10–2 with that of Figure 10–1. The applicant is obviously one whose work experience is a stronger asset than is prior education. Also, an equivalent position in another, larger firm appears to be the goal of the applicant. Generally when a person in a job is interested in a job change, he or she should withhold the list of references until an interview is held and serious consideration for the person is apparent.

SUMMARY

The task of finding a first job after graduation or of seeking a beneficial job change should be a serious one and is often time consuming. Whether you fall in either of these categories or neither, you will find that maintaining an up-to-date personal record is valuable. Just as most people take the time to assess their monetary net worth from time to time, they should assess their personal worth. You might find you are worth more than you imagined. Finally, once your data sheet is complete, proofread it carefully. If you were an employer, would you be pleased to receive the data sheet you have prepared? All the thinking that went into it will pay dividends as you proceed to write the letter to accompany it.

Chapter 11

WRITING APPLICATION LETTERS

The application letter follows the basic salesletter plan—getting attention and interest, identifying specific preparation to do a job, giving sufficient evidence to be convincing, and asking for action. The primary difference is in the product you have to sell. Instead of selling a *thing*, you are selling your own *merits*. But in either case, you're selling an idea—you have what the recipient needs.

As indicated earlier, the writing task is simplified if you have preceded it with a thorough job- and self-analysis. And for most of us, the writing is almost sure to be more effective if we first review some of the important aspects of composition discussed in Chapters 2, 3, and 4: coherence, concreteness, convention, emphasis, originality, simplicity, sincerity, and empathy.

Knowing the basics of composition is certainly helpful in composing application letters. But knowing them and even applying them well do not assure an effective letter. The following list illustrates some of the common errors made by applicants:

Copying a letter written by some other person.
Writing as if the letter were an autobiography.
Overworking "I," "me," and "my."
Sounding unduly humble.
Begging or asking for sympathy.
Sounding too flippant or casual.
Seeming to lecture the recipient.
Seeming to brag about accomplishments.
Writing "I'm qualified" without giving evidence to support the statement.
Using the present employer's stationery.
Commenting negatively about the present employer.

Writing about graduation as if it were the only requisite needed.

Using vague, general terms.

Repeating (instead of interpreting) résumé information.

Using outworn expressions.

The following words and expressions have been overused in application letters. Try to avoid them.

Applicant. If your letter shows how you are suited to do the work, you need not label yourself as an "applicant." To do so is to say the obvious.

Application. Your letter will be identified as an application without this label.

Consider me as an applicant for the position. Indicate this idea through implication. Space is important. Use it to show you can do the job.

I should like to apply for. . . . Just apply. No need to say you "would like" to apply or "are applying."

Interview. Let your competitors use this expression. It connotes a formal, question-and-answer session. This word is very common in the final paragraph. A careful writer can introduce the *idea* of an interview without using the word. "Talk with you," "discuss the work," and "call at your office" are possibilities.

Position. To some people, a *position* is a title or post that someone holds; it doesn't necessarily apply to work. Use *job* or *work* if you want to sound more original and more realistic.

Qualifications. Others use this word too much. Employers will recognize training and experience as "qualifications" without your attaching the label. You can usually leave the word to implication or use such words as *preparation, background,* or *work record.*

Let's examine some parts of application letters written for different job-getting occasions—unsolicited application letters, solicited application letters, and other letters about employment.

THE UNSOLICITED APPLICATION LETTER

For several reasons, firms like to receive applications for jobs they have not advertised. With a file of unsolicited applications, a firm can achieve several objectives: (1) save advertising costs; (2) fill jobs more quickly, because the personnel department can look in the file and be in touch with an applicant in a short time; (3) save personnel department time, because the department may find a suitable worker from a small file of unsolicited letters; otherwise, an advertisement may bring fifty or a hundred invited applications, all of which require some attention; (4) avoid possible goodwill-losing situations, because some who have applied may be embittered when they are not employed; (5) get applicants who possess the qualities of initiative and foresight; (6) be fairly certain that any present employee who may not be measuring up to performance standards can be replaced.

From the applicant's point of view, the unsolicited application letter also has advantages: (1) It increases the number of jobs from which the applicant can select. (2) It meets with less competition than it would have if it were sent in response to an advertisement. (3) It could *create* a job if it persuaded the employer to believe that a worker was needed to do something that is not now being done. (4) It may assist in getting a better job, because the highly preferred jobs are often filled before any applications are invited. (5) It may suggest initiative on the part of the writer.

Basically, the unsolicited letter of application is a sales letter. As such, it follows the fundamental steps of selling—getting attention, arousing interest, presenting convincing evidence, and asking for action.

Getting attention and interest. In application letters, the choice of attention getters is more limited than in sales letters. Consider the following possibilities.

1. Presenting outstanding qualifications: "When you need a secretary who can type 70 words per minute, take shorthand at 125, and transcribe at 50, please call me."
2. Describing job requirements: " 'Trainee must have college degree with major in finance and economics, and excellent references.' Please check to see how well my background fits these trainee specifications, as listed in your Information Booklet No. 45!"
3. Referring to the source of job information. "From the *Gazette's* July 13 story about your plans to market pork on the West Coast, I concluded that you may want to hire a well-trained, experienced meat salesman."
4. Using the name of someone in the organization. "Dr. Allan Porter

of your Market Research Department told our fraternity last month that you often add young marketing majors to your summer sales force."

5. Using a catch phrase that leads to the presentation of qualifications. " 'A blind man is driving this car.' That sign on the back of one of your representative's cars opened my eyes. I'm no longer blind to the fact that you are selling four fifths of the venetian blinds sold in Springburg. May I help you?"

The possibilities for attention-getting devices have by no means been exhausted. Regardless of the manner in which you seek to attract attention, your attention-getting paragraph should let the employer know he is about to read an application for a specific job or a specific type of work. The first paragraph should lead naturally into a discussion of preparation for the job.

Presenting preparation. If you can get attention by summarizing your outstanding qualification in the very first sentence, fine. Then you should proceed to give the supporting details. But if you use some other attention getter, you will need to introduce your qualifications as quickly as possible. The natural tendency is to plunge into an historical account of past experiences, as the following second paragraph does:

> While I was a student at Wilcoy High School, I majored in business subjects—bookkeeping, salesmanship, and business law. Then after studying business for two years at Hays Business College, I took a job as collection agent with Porter and Sons, where I am still employed.

Perhaps many applicants use this approach because it is narrative. Sequence of ideas is easy because the applicant writes about experiences in chronological order. But the disadvantages of the narrative approach probably outweigh the advantages. Remember, the reader wants to know whether you can do the job for which you are applying. You are probably a stranger, and your autobiography may sound very much like hundreds of others. Then, too, the narrative approach is conducive to using too many "I's." Remember the admonition to write to others in terms of their own interests. The reader is primarily interested in the phase of your experience most related to the job. And you are expected to point out that relationship. Does the preceding example tell anything not included on the résumé? Observe that the following paragraph concentrates on *interpreting* the résumé instead of *repeating* it.

> From the business courses taken in school and from two years' experience as a collection agent, I have wrestled with a variety of human-relations problems—legal, psychological, and sales promotional. The claims adjusters in your department almost certainly have the same types of problems—acting always within the limits of law and ethics, saying words most likely to influence a particular client, and constantly promoting the company.

Notice that the preceding paragraph employs "I" only once; it does not mention the factual details about where the applicant went to school, the courses taken, or the location of the present job. These facts can be included in the résumé. Notice, too, that the emphasis is not on chronology. Rather, it is on the relationship of the applicant's experience to the requirements of the job. Furthermore, the paragraph gives the impression that this applicant knows what would be expected of a claims adjuster. And this point comes across without lecturing or boasting. The last sentence is long, but it is not too complicated for easy reading.

In the discussion of your background, you can sometimes weave something into your writing to show that you are familiar with the firm and its future plans or present problems. But don't put yourself in the position of telling that which is already known, as the following sentence does:

> In addition to opening three new branches this year, your bank is installing drive-in windows in all its branches and switching to electronic calculating machines.

The sentence does little more than reveal a knowledge of company affairs. Use an indirect method of revealing this knowledge; let this information appear in a sentence that says something more important:

> In addition to taking finance courses and working part time as a teller at the ABC Bank, I'm just completing an eight-week course in the programing of the XXX computer—the same model State Bank (the bank to which this application is being sent) is now making preparations to install.

The preceding paragraph could profitably continue with some details about the course just completed—significant subject matter covered, most important concepts the applicant came to understand and appreciate, projects undertaken, names of guest speakers if they were well known, and so forth. From a desire to be brief, or from sheer laziness, too many applicants would omit such details. Rationalizing, they would argue that the reader is a busy person and does not want to read a long letter. But remember, the reader's task of finding the right employee for the job is a serious one. Instead of being resented, the details are appreciated; they illustrate vividly the relationship between the applicant's background and the job. In addition, the applicant who presents such details implies knowledge of what the job entails and the requisites for success in it. Many are the applicants who will be satisfied to reveal that they have "had a course in" or "majored in" a subject; but, without supporting details, a reader can hardly judge whether anything was *learned.*

Asking for action. As in a sales letter, writers of application letters define for themselves the desired action before beginning to write. Whether they want the employer to grant an immediate interview, give some indication of interest, or file the application for future openings, they write with that action in mind. Naturally, they define that action in the final paragraph. They may want the employer to *call* (the number is on the résumé) or to *write.* Either of these specific words would be better than the general word *contact.*

For the ending paragraph, keep the following suggestions in mind: (1) Mention the specific action you want; just ask for it, don't demand it. (2) Try to sound natural and original; too many letters end with a trite expression, such as "May I have an interview at your convenience." (3) Express gratitude because you are asking a favor, but use first person and future tense instead of the present "Thank you for calling. . . ." or the presumptuous "Thank you in advance." (4) Try to work in a final reference to the most outstanding feature of your preparation for the job; this final reference adds *emphasis* because of its last-paragraph position, and it shows *coherence* because of its relationship to the preceding discussion. It also indicates *unity* because of its tie-in with the first sentence. It makes the whole letter now seem complete, as does the following closing paragraph:

> Please examine the attached data sheet and write to the references. Then, I wish you would call me to suggest a time when we could discuss the possibility of putting my collection experience to work for you.

Now that we have examined the major parts of an unsolicited letter of application, let's examine a complete letter. The following letter is not presented as a "model"; regard it as a letter illustrating the application of principles discussed previously. (Since this application was signed by a man, the masculine pronoun is used in the commentary.)

Part-time writing for a collection agency and a year's university instruction in business writing—please check to see how well these experiences prepare me for entrance into your Correspondence Services Section.

Seeks attention by mentioning the most pertinent features of the applicant's background. Since the experience was considered more likely to influence the reader, it is presented before university instruction is presented. Since he speaks of "entrance," he doesn't expect to begin at the top. He's realistic. He knows he will have to prove himself before being given a more responsible position. By using the exact name of the correspondence section, he reveals some knowledge of the firm.

When you need a new sales series to promote your new Perfecto 301, an individual adjustment refusal, or a new collection series, you could have me prepare them; I have worked with all three types.

Talks of doing something to solve the employer's problems. The applicant must have analyzed the relationship between preparation and job requirements. He must know that, in this section, writers are called upon to write various types of letters. Through his own initiative or observation, he has learned about the 301 promotional campaign.

My school writing courses included the writing and criticizing of all types of letters. We analyzed letters from every angle.

Reveals the applicant did *something in the school courses. Many applicants would have simply said they* had *them.*

My sales letters seemed to be most effective when I chose a central theme and stuck with it, placing the product in the prospect's hands and describing the benefits he got from using it.

Indicates he learned *something in the courses. And he reminds the reader of what he learned without preaching or lecturing. He talks the language of a sales writer—"prospect," "central theme," and "product."*

Both students and teachers were very critical of my refusal-adjustment letters until I started giving the reasons behind refusals, then following with a logical refusal and an attempt to preserve goodwill.

Makes no pretense of perfection. He improved his writing as a result of criticism; he's not afraid of it. He is willing to learn. He's tactfully revealing some knowledge of the proper technique for good adjustment writing—without seeming to lecture. And he's still using the language of the job.

As a part-time worker in Maxwell's Collections Department while earning my B.S. degree, I helped Mr. Albert Smith prepare an entire collection series. We know how much hard work goes into such a writing project; we know the pleasures that goes with it, too.

Does not repeat information given on the data sheet, but interprets it. Since the job is as likely to entail collection writing as any other type, he provides evidence of his ability to write collection letters, too. He establishes his graduation, but notice how it is de-emphasized. He knows graduation never made a writer of anyone.

Suggests he can work with other people—"we know . . ." he knows that writing is not play—it's a serious business. But he likes his work, probably because he is successful. He is not likely to quit on the spur of the moment for some other type of work.

Mr. Smith tells me this year's loss from bad debts is almost one percent less than last year's, and he thinks the new letters are primarily responsible. Would you like to see them?

Presents evidence (which can be verified by calling Maxwell's) of his effectiveness without seeming to judge himself or to brag. He shares the success with Mr. Smith, and he isn't so naive as to rule out the possibility of another variable's influence. Shows willingness to substantiate his claims with proof. Maybe the reader will suggest he bring the letters along when he comes for a personal discussion. The sentence serves as a good transition into the action ending.

Please study the attached data sheet and call or write to the references.

Delays reference to the résumé until he has completed his talking points. He refers to his résumé in a sentence that also says something else, and he avoids the obvious remark, "References are listed on. . . ."

I shall appreciate your writing me to name a time when we can talk over the correspondence work you have to do and the correspondence work I have done.

Expresses gratitude in first person to make it emphatic. Tells the action wanted. Uses informal language ("Talk over") instead of the formal ("interview"). Uses "work" as a mild reminder of his desire to perform instead of hold a position. Includes a

> *final reminder of his basic correspondence experiences, which are essential for entrance into the correspondence services section.*

When placed on a standard-size sheet of stationery, the preceding letter fills one page. A shorter letter would hardly have afforded the opportunity to illustrate the extent of versatility in correspondence work.

The preceding letter makes no mention of salary. That problem can be discussed later. To discuss salary in the initial application letter is to risk magnifying its importance.

Neither does the letter reveal why the applicant wants to leave the job now held nor why the addressee has been selected as a prospective employer. To include too many subsidiary details is to de-emphasize qualifications. An applicant cannot hope to answer all questions in the letter; some are most appropriately discussed in the interview. In some job-getting situations, the letter of application is actually preceded by an interview during which the letter is invited.

THE SOLICITED APPLICATION LETTER

Whether your application letter is solicited or unsolicited, the principles of presenting qualifications are the same. The primary difference is the beginning paragraph. In the solicited letter, no attention-getting device is necessary. The firm is already devoting some attention to filling its vacancies. You already have a contact. The preferred way is to start with the contact (the source of the invitation) and proceed from there. A good beginning for an invited application will ordinarily (1) refer to the source of the invitation, (2) indicate the specific job for which the candidate applies, and (3) suggest the candidate's major qualifications. The following examples illustrate:

> As you requested in our discussion yesterday, I have prepared the attached résumé of my educational and experience background for cost-accounting work.

or

> Because of my three years' military experience as a personnel man and several college courses in personnel administration, I believe you will be interested in my application for the personnel post you advertised in this morning's *Daily News.*

In responses to blind ads, follow the principles that apply to other solicited application letters. But keep in mind that the advertiser has placed you in a rather awkward position by not telling you the name and location of the business. Without these details, you may have difficulty matching your preparation with the job. You may want to give a reserved response. For example, you may not want to give references, but just indicate a willingness to supply them on request. You don't want your references to receive requests from firms with whom you would not care to work.

If the blind ad asks you to state the salary expected, you will have to mention salary in some way. Perhaps the best way is to say you are willing to accept the standard or customary salary paid for the job, or that you would like to discuss the salary with the interviewer. The employer places you in an awkward position when he asks you to state a salary even though you don't know the precise duties or circumstances that surround the job.

OTHER LETTERS ABOUT EMPLOYMENT

Other job-connected letters include job-inquiry letters, application follow-ups, job acceptances, job refusals, and thank-you letters.

Job-inquiry letters are sometimes mailed when applicants know the firm will not officially regard them as applicants until they fill out an application form. In that case, they may write to request a form. Although the request for the form is fairly routine, candidates increase their chances of getting the form if they at least give enough information about themselves to assure the personnel department that they have some of the requisites for the job mentioned. For example:

> May I please have an application form for work in your actuarial department. I am finishing my college work, which includes several courses in mathematics, statistics, and insurance.
>
> We plan to make our home in your city after school is out in June.

Such a letter can hardly be more effective than a complete letter of application; it can be less effective. But, because of its directness and shortness, it does enable the candidate to make job contacts that would probably not be made otherwise. Especially if the applicant wanted a position for which applicants were relatively scarce, some sort of response would be almost certain.

Application follow-ups can be well worth the time required to write them. If within a short time candidates do not receive a response to their application, they might reinforce it with a second letter. By so doing, they (1) keep the file active, (2) report additional experiences that prepare them for the job, and (3) create an impression of diligence—of knowing what they want and going after it methodically:

> Since I wrote to you about a junior accounting position in January, I have completed three additional courses in accounting and have been doing some part-time individual income-tax work for Mr. Hugo Smith of this city.
>
> Please keep my application in the active file and let me know when you need another junior accountant.

Job-acceptance letters are easy letters to write. As in other letters that convey good news, they begin by accepting the job in the very first sentence, follow with any necessary details, and end naturally with a pleasant look toward the time when the employee is to report for work:

> I accept your offer of a job in the Accounts Payable Department.
>
> Here are the security-clearance forms and health record. I shall bring a photostatic copy of my birth certificate when I report for work on Monday morning, July 1.
>
> Thank you for introducing me to some of the accountants when I talked with you last week. I shall enjoy working with them.

Job-refusal letters follow the inductive sequence—reasons first, then the refusal, and a pleasant ending. When the job we wanted goes to some other candidate, we want to know about it and we want some justification. Employers are the same way. They like to know as quickly as possible whether a job offer has been accepted; and, if possible, they would like to know the reasons why a job offer has been declined. As a matter of courtesy, we should tell them. We should be tactful because we may want a job with the firm later:

> Yours was one of the most interesting job interviews I had in my search for tax accounting work. I especially remember your ideas on the percentage-depletion problem.
>
> As you pointed out, opportunities in Petrolio are exceedingly good for those who are primarily interested in costs. But since my major interest is in tax accounting, I have taken a job with Mills Mining Company where my responsibilities will be restricted to tax accounting.
>
> I appreciate the time you spent with me.

The first sentence lets the personnel man know the candidate had other interviews—a good way to lead up to the statement of his accepting a job with another company. In the second sentence, the applicant reminds the reader of knowledge gained in the interview—a compliment to the interviewer. After these remarks come the reason for the refusal, the refusal (stated in polite, positive language), and an expression of gratitude.

Thank-you letters following an interview are appropriate, even when applicants think they have no chance for the job. After an interviewer has indicated there is no chance for the job, the candidate still owes the interviewer an expression of gratitude:

> I certainly appreciated your taking time to talk with me last week about the job in your data-processing department.
>
> As you suggested, I am enrolling in a computer course this summer. Later, after my knowledge and skill have improved, I would be glad to talk with you again.

An employer who receives such a letter would no doubt react something like this: "This applicant recognizes his weaknesses and he is doing something about them. I'll keep him in mind."

Many competitors for a job will neglect this small courtesy of sending a thank-you note. The simple expression of gratitude could decide the case in the applicant's favor:

> I appreciate the time you took to talk with me today.
>
> After your discussion of service-attitude in selling, I was glad I had chosen selling for my career. You sold me on the Farnsworth Company.
>
> Thank you very much.

In each of the thank-you examples cited, the candidate reveals that something is *remembered* from the interview. That's a more original way to please the interviewer than to say you "enjoyed" the interview. Observe, too, that the thank-you letters are relatively short. Presenting too much of anything else de-emphasizes the gratitude.

SUMMARY

The letter of application is a sales letter that sells you! Its goal is to secure an interview in which you can continue to sell yourself. Meticulous effort should go into the entire application. In the preceding discussions of letters and résumés, not much has been said about grammar, spelling, punctuation, and typing. Check to see whether errors appear. Those who read applications naturally assume their authors have done their best. To allow errors to appear is to risk a reader's interpreting them as evidence of ignorance, disrespect, haste, or carelessness—negative characteristics that could carry over into a person's work as an employee. On the other hand, a well prepared application can only indicate positive qualities.

Chapter 12

THE REPORT PROCESS AND RESEARCH METHODS

Although the business letter is written and planned to achieve a desired action to the news conveyed, the business report is written and planned to transmit objective information logically and concisely. In essence, a report is a logical document, and a letter is a psychologically designed message. This chapter and several following are intended to give an overview of report processes and preparation.

THE NATURE OF BUSINESS REPORTS

A report is a written or oral message used (1) to convey business information about status or research from one area of an organization to another to assist the decision-making function or (2) to present a solution to a problem. The profit-and-loss statement, balance sheet, daily stock averages, market analyses and other forms of business information are reports. So too are internal memoranda showing production figures, work progress, and employee turnover.

As a matter of practice, management should request only reports that are needed. Many in business consider routine reports as "busy work." Perhaps these people are actually uninformed about the ultimate application of their work. The growth of business information systems came about to increase and improve the flow of report-type information to management. It seems that management never has enough information. When information is needed, we can be assured that the need arises because of a problem. Thus, the real basis for a report is its contribution to problem solving.

Some recurrent problems call for a constant flow of information; other problems are unique and call for information on a one-time basis. If we can, therefore, accept the business problem as the underlying reason for all report writing, the preparation, organization, and writing become much easier. We can pinpoint the specific need and use of the information.

The logical steps in problem solving are the following, and they apply to report preparation:

1. Recognize and define the problem.
2. Select a method of solution.
3. Collect and analyze data.
4. Arrive at an answer to the problem.

It is important to remember that these steps all take place normally before any attempt is made to put a written report in final form. Let's take a closer look at these four preliminary steps to successful report writing.

RECOGNIZE AND DEFINE THE PROBLEM

Pinpoint the problem to be solved. Take a good look at the instructions accompanying the report request. Attempt to divide the major request into subrequests such as "What, why, when, where, and who?" The solutions of the parts may lead to the solution of the major problem. The *what* and *why* are the important questions. Unless we know what is wanted, it is difficult to explain why. The opposite is also true. Once these two elements are identified, write them down. The problem is on its way to solution.

At this point, laboratory scientists would establish an hypothesis—a tentative solution which they would attempt to prove or disprove. But the early definition and analysis of the problem would have given the study direction.

Hypotheses may be stated in either of two ways, positively or in null style. A positive hypothesis is stated to indicate a definite bias toward a conclusion as in: Production of employees will increase if employees are given added pay for production in excess of the standard. This hypothesis, it is claimed, shows the researcher's bias toward the conclusion. It could be advanced also that the researcher would be susceptible to treating data in such a way as to lead to that conclusion.

In sophisticated research, an hypothesis is often stated in null fashion to attempt to eliminate a stated bias as in: No significant difference will exist between production of workers on an incentive pay plan and those on a regular pay plan. Although not all business research is amenable to hypothesis testing, the concept of using hypotheses is valuable in terms of maintaining an objective view by the researcher.

SELECT A METHOD OF SOLUTION

Four commonly used research methods are available for the solution of problems:

1. Library research.
2. Normative survey research.
3. Observational research.
4. Experimental research.

Library research is a part of all studies. It saves a researcher the trouble of "reinventing the wheel." By searching for already-developed information on a problem, one can save much time and effort. Because the boundaries of knowledge in any given field are constantly expanding, library research is necessary to establish "what is" at any given time. New research, then, adds to the boundaries. Applied to business research, the library method involves the investigation of books, periodicals, and any records stored by the business. Because it concerns itself with material already created, library research contributes second-hand data, and library materials are described as "secondary sources."

In undertaking library research, keep in mind two suggestions. First, protect yourself against collecting too much information. You can do this by taking notes as you proceed rather than by attempting to collect entire articles, books, or reports. Second, preserve your integrity. Do this by making bibliography references on each source used. A bibliographical reference consists of the following: Author's name, title of article or book, volume or publisher and page number(s) of materials used. For example:

Chase, Stuart. *The Power of Words.* New York: Harcourt, Brace and World, Inc., 1954, p. 84.

Normative survey research is a method used to determine the status of something at the time of the research—hence, the term "normative" which describes norms or standards. This method most often uses questionnaires or interviews for gathering data. The United States Census and Gallup political polls are examples.

In all surveys, an assumption is made that the people surveyed are either representative of a larger group or constitute the entire population to be studied. When the survey covers only a portion of the entire population on which generalizations are to be drawn, the portion surveyed is called a "sample." Obviously, care must be taken to assure that the sample is really representative of the population. Here are some suggestions for questionnaire or interview surveys:

1. Test the wording of your items with others before preparing the final survey instrument. Test their answers to assure understanding.
2. Try to ask for easily recalled information.
3. Begin with the easiest item. The questionnaire may end up in the waste basket otherwise.
4. Make responding easy. Items which can be answered simply by checking an appropriate place are best.
5. Group items by subject or area if possible. You'll help the respondent stay on track.
6. Provide adequate instructions to assure consistency in replies.
7. Develop a format that will make your job of tabulating replies easy. A little more time spent preparing the questionnaire may save much time in later handling the data.
8. If you use mail questionnaires, enclose a stamped return envelope.

Observational research, or statistical research, is used here to describe research involving statistical analysis of data. Suppose, for example, that you wanted to know if scores on an aptitude test had a relationship to grades made in a college course. You would gather grades and test scores on each student, perform statistical correlations, and draw conclusions from the analysis. Frequently, market surveys use both survey and observational research to determine buying habits of income groups

The name observational research is used because this type of analysis observes phenomena to assist in establishing new principles.

Experimental research is familiar to most of us as the test-tube research conducted in a laboratory. Experimental research involves two samples having exactly the same ingredients under the same conditions before a variable is added to one of the samples. The differences then identified are due to the variable. As a simple example, assume an office has a great number of clerk-typists doing the same routine tasks. Management decides to make a study of the effect of incentive pay on production. It separates the clerk-typists into two groups equal in experience, skill, and previous production rates. One group is then placed on incentive pay. During the length of the study, the difference in production is noted. Because the incentive pay is assumed to be the only variable, the difference is attributed to its influence.

Although experimental research is difficult to adapt to human activities, the point is that it can be used by management just as the laboratory scientist uses it. Along with library, survey, and observational research, experimental research completes the available research methods. No matter what problem serves as the basis for a report, we must use one or a combination of these methods to solve the problem.

COLLECT AND ORGANIZE THE DATA

Having decided on the plan, the researcher must outline a step-by-step approach to the solution of the problem. Because the human mind is inquisitive, given a desirable tangent, it will wander off into ephermeral daydreams. Such trips to dreamland distract from the job at hand; and if given free reign, they can lend to obliteration of the object of the study.

Therefore, keep on the right track. Plan your attack and follow it. Question every step you take for its contribution to your objective. Keep a record of your actions. A criterion for good research is whether another qualified researcher could take the report of research, conduct the same study, and arrive at the same conclusions. Thus, sufficient detail on procedures should be included to permit a similar study to be made.

Use such techniques as a card system to reduce library findings to workable size. Through tabulation techniques, quantitative data included on a vast number of questionnaires can be reduced. As shown

FIGURE 12–1
The report process

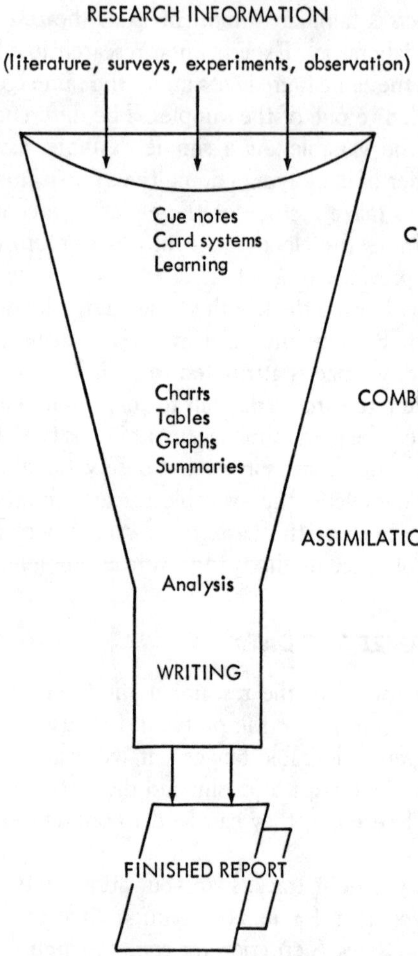

in Figure 12–1, the report process is one of reducing original information to a convenient size that can be handled in a written message. The following steps are suggested:

1. Evaluate each item of information for its usefulness.
2. Reduce the useful information through cue notes (the shortest

thing you can write that will aid in recall of a larger amount), card systems, or memory.
3. Combine like information into understandable form through the use of graphics or tables or written summaries.
4. Report in written form your analysis of the data.

ARRIVE AT AN ANSWER TO THE PROBLEM

At this final stage in the solution of a problem, report writers have the results of their research before them in concise form. They are able to see the problem in its entirety. Following the step-by-step plan, researchers collected and organized information in usable form. When properly taken, these steps should lead to a logical answer to the problem.

Sound answers or conclusions, however, are unlikely if interpretation is faulty. Some common mental errors can seriously affect the interpretation of data:

1. Trying, consciously or unconsciously, to make results conform to a prediction or desire.
2. Hoping for spectacular results. Unfounded, revolutionary conclusions can negatively affect the researcher's future credibility.
3. Attempting to compare when commonality is absent. Concluding that a certain product would sell well in Montana because it sold well in Florida would be risky.
4. Assuming a cause-effect relationship when one does not exist. A new sales manager may have been in office one year and sales may have doubled. The doubling might have been in spite of, rather than because of, the new sales manager.
5. Failing to consider important factors and thus basing conclusions on lack of evidence. Simply because "we have had no complaints about our refund policy" is not necessarily evidence the policy is good. Has anyone applied for a refund?
6. Assuming a constancy of human behavior. In the 1980 election, people changed their minds or made them up at the last minute; public opinion polls taken only a few days earlier were completely inaccurate.

SUMMARY

Good researchers attempt to consider all factors, and they recognize and identify possible limitations to their research. Throughout the entire four-step problem-solving method, they attempt to protect themselves not only against their own human failings but also against their material. That is the nature of research. Your own success as a report writer will rest on your ability to reason objectively and to write accurately.

Chapter 13

ORGANIZING REPORTS

As we have just learned, the report itself is written only after the following four steps in the problem solving process have been completed:

1. Recognize and define the problem.
2. Select a method of solution.
3. Collect and organize the data.
4. Arrive at an answer to the original problem.

THE REPORT OUTLINING PROCESS

Obviously, if these steps form the basis for a study, they can also serve as the basis for organizing the report. Rephrased, the steps could become headings for a report outline:

1. The problem.
2. Method used.
3. Findings.
4. Conclusion.

Logically, the report would then tell the reader what the problem was in the first section, detail the method or methods used in the second section, report what was found in the third, and end with the answer to the problem or the conclusions.

Because the findings and the conclusions are of most importance to both the researcher and the reader, they receive the greatest attention in the written presentation. The definition of the problem and detail of the method used are of secondary interest in most business studies. To place emphasis on findings and conclusions, then, the outline may be changed to give the problem and method relatively minor status to findings and conclusions as in the following:

I. Introduction.
   A. Statement of the problem.
   B. Description of the method and sources used.
II. Findings.
III. Conclusions and/or recommendations.

This outline includes all four items, but by combining the problem and method in one section, it gives relatively greater importance to the sections devoted to one item—the findings and conclusions. But these headings could make pretty dull reading. Keep in mind that the items in the outline will later become headings and subheadings in a report. In long reports, they might well become items on the familiar "Table of Contents" page. Let's take a hypothetical problem, assume we've done the research, and plan an outline for the written report.

Here's the problem. The XYZ Company is considering the purchase of a corporate airplane to replace a ten-year-old one. You are to prepare a report presenting an analysis of three possible new planes—the Jetstar, the Rover, and the Skylark. You've studied trade-in allowances, prices, range, speed, operating costs, and safety factors. Also, you had opinions from two company pilots and six company executives who took test rides. After much consideration, and much arithmetic, you know you are going to recommend the Jetstar. Thus, your outline could take this form:

I. Introduction.
   A. Problem.
   B. Method and sources.
II. Performance factors of three planes.
   A. The Jetstar.
   B. The Rover.
   C. The Skylark.
III. Conclusions and recommendations.

Something is missing, however. What criteria were used in making the selection? Performance is covered, but what about price and opinions of the pilots and executives. It is evident that the report will include, according to this outline, a complete statement about all the features of the Jetstar and follow with similar statements about the Rover and the Skylark. Consider the difficulty of the reader in trying to make comparisons when items being compared are not presented together in the report. For example, comparison would be easy if the cost of each plane were presented in the same section. Using criteria as divisions in the report makes the presentation much more effective. Note how the following improved outline uses criteria rather than names of planes for report divisions.

I. Introduction.
   A. The problem.
   B. The method and sources.
II. Cost and trade-in favor the Jetstar.
III. Range and speed are comparable in the three planes.
IV. Executives prefer Jetstar's comfort.
V. Pilots like the Jetstar and Rover.
VI. XYZ should purchase the Jetstar.

Notice that items II to V are actually subdivisions of the findings and item VI is the conclusion and recommendation section. The language used also describes the contents of each section. Descriptive headings such as these are commonly called "talking headings." As shown below, this outline becomes a contents page simply by adding page numbers. Because of the organization, even the Roman numerals and letters can be omitted.

Introduction 1
   The problem 1
   The method 1
Cost and trade-in favor the Jetstar 2
Range and speed are comparable in the
   three planes 4
Executives prefer Jetstar's comfort 6
Pilots like the Jetstar and Rover 8
XYZ should purchase the Jetstar 10

The report writer has an option about outlining style. Because people expect the beginning of a report to be the introduction, the introductory headings might be omitted. In that case, the preceding outline would begin with the heading about cost and trade-in as shown here:

Cost and trade-in favor the Jetstar 2
Range and speed are comparable in the
three planes 4
Executives prefer Jetstar's comfort 6
Pilots like the Jetstar and Rover 8
XYZ should purchase the Jetstar 10

The content about statement of the problem and method of solution would not be different in the two reports. Only the headings would be removed in the second example.

THE SCOPE OF OUTLINING

To this point, reports have been considered from a formal point of view. That is, we have talked pretty much about reports as being presentations of a highly sophisticated nature. The report process was built around a problem to be solved, the method of solving it, and what to do with the material gathered. This process led to an outline, to possible headings in a report, and then to a theoretical table of contents. Not all reports require this much attention to outlining.

The sophistication of the report and the detail put into it depend on two factors: (1) the purpose of the report, and (2) the amount of presentation necessary to serve the purpose. Various classifications of reports have evolved in business and have labels attached to them, such as internal-external reports, progress reports, periodic reports, financial reports, annual reports and so on. Regardless of the label, a business report is an organized, objective communication of information which assists in the solution of a business problem.

The most useful classification of reports involves the formality or sophistication involved in presentation. All reports would fall on a formal-informal continuum as shown in Figure 13–1.

We have shown business research in the center of the continuum primarily because it can extend from one extreme to the other. Complex problems deserve more detail and hence more formality than simple

FIGURE 13–1

Formal — Informal

Scientific research

Business research

Routine communications

problems. The needs of the reader of the report also help determine the degree of formality. Some executives prefer a straightforward, casual style; some desire great detail and formal writing; some shun statistical data, and others thrive on it. Thus, business probably has as many degrees of formality as there are types of readers and writers.

The interoffice memorandum, for example, may be short with the only outline needed being the appropriate subject line. Toward the formal end of the continuum lies the hypothetical outline prepared for the report on the study of the three airplanes covered earlier. In that study, the formal outline was developed only after all the research findings had been gathered and analyzed. Keep this in mind: Outlining and writing are processes that take place after you know generally what your findings mean and what your conclusion will be. The outline is simply a guide for the writing task. The more writing involved, the greater the need for outlining.

The outline establishes the sequence of items in the report. A good outline also helps the writer make sense of his material. To the writer, then, creating order from disorder, even chaos, is the function of outlining. Outlining is a mental task, and though no magic formula applies, an understanding of some outline symbols is helpful in the process.

OUTLINE SYMBOLS

Styles of outline symbols other than the Roman numeral type are increasing in usage. The use of symbols helps systematize material to be classified and organized. For example, the Dewey Decimal System used in libraries contributes to an outline of man's knowledge. This system has a great advantage over others in that it is expandable. Depite the tremendous increase in publications since Dewey developed it over 100 years ago, the system has been able to accommodate the volume. Along with the Library of Congress system, it is used in all libraries in the country.

Although such a sophisticated system is not required in report outlining, the logic of a system of symbols leads to effective organization. In Figure 13–2, note the similarity of outline symbols.

Note that the Roman numeral item IA2, the decimal item 1.12, and the alphanumeric item A1b are used to designate the same item in the three outlines. Roman numeral outlines are used widely in schools and industry, decimal outlines are found frequently in engineering and other technically oriented fields, and variations of the alphanumeric

FIGURE 13–2

Roman numeral	*Decimal*	*Alphanumeric*
I.	1.0	A.
A.	1.1	1.
1.	1.11	*a.*
2.	1.12	*b.*
B.	1.2	2.
II.	2.0	B.

outline are used by many governmental organizations. All are valuable aids. The symbol system helps the writer plan in a logical way and is expandable in that additional subdivisions can be created without disrupting the basic outline.

In report writing, most items in the outline ultimately become subheadings in the report itself. These headings are described as "degree" headings as in the following example using the Roman numeral outline:

I. First degree
  A. Second degree
    1. Third degree
      a. Fourth degree
      b. Fourth degree
    2. Third degree
  B. Second degree
II. First degree

Each of these degrees in the outline is the result of dividing or classifying. The thing divided or classified is the whole of the information available. For example, an outline of the United States might be prepared by a geographic classification of the individual states as follows:

I. The United States
  A. Northeastern states
    1. Maine
    2. Massachusetts
    3. New Hampshire
    4. Etc.
  B. Northcentral states
    1. Illinois
    2. Michigan
    3. Etc.
  C. . . .

As you divide the whole into comparable parts, you arrive at second-degree classifications. Dividing the second-degree classifications into comparable parts leads to third-degree classifications, and so on. A major principle in outline preparation is that any part must be divided into at least two parts or it should not be divided. For example, if part A does not have at least subheads 1 and 2, it should not be divided. Remember, too, that all but the most elaborate reports probably do not go beyond the third- or fourth-degree headings.

At the most formal level, the report may consist of several parts. The judgment of the person preparing the report will, of course, determine what parts are necessary using the criteria of size, complexity, and reader requirements.

DEDUCTIVE-INDUCTIVE ORGANIZATION

The overall report organization will take either a direct, deductive format or an indirect, inductive format. For example, will the report reader be better informed if the conclusions of the report are given first or delayed to the end of the report.

The four-step method of problem solving is an inductive or indirect method. After determining the purpose, using a method of research, gathering and analyzing the findings, the researcher arrives at a conclusion. This process is indirect because it progresses through all the steps before arriving at a conclusion. To write the report in this sequence delays the conclusion to the end. On the other hand, a direct approach would be to present the conclusion at the beginning of the report and support it with the details of the research. Schematically, these two approaches to organization appear as follows:

Deductive or direct	*Inductive or indirect*
Conclusion	Details
Details	Conclusion.

You will recall from the chapters on letter writing and planning that favorable information is communicated deductively and unfavorable information is best communicated inductively. The criterion for selecting a report plan is not the same as for letters, however. Whether the news is favorable or unfavorable is not necessarily important to report organization. Executives are busy and want their reading made as easy as possible. In long reports, the deductive plan is achieved by presenting a capsule overview of the report as an introductory part. In short reports, the deductive organization involves simply beginning the report with the conclusion.

FORMAL REPORT PARTS

The interoffice memorandum is the simplest of business reports. However, something interesting happens to it. As the memo incorporates more and more material, headings appear, dividing the material into logical sections. When the memo grows to several pages, the writer decides to add a transmittal memorandum as a first page. If he or she deems it helpful, the writer adds a content outline. At this point, a title page may be developed. Then raw data or bibliography items appear as addenda at the end of the memo. Then the item that began as a simple memo becomes a full-blown report.

All these things are not "padding" to make the report impressive; they are incorporated to help the reader. The complete formal report may include the following parts:

1. Letter of transmittal.
2. Title page.
3. Contents page.
4. Synopsis or summary.
5. Body.
6. Addenda.

Item 5, the body, is the core of the report. It presents the purpose, method, findings, and conclusion. The other items are all add-ons to assist understanding. It is interesting how the simple memo grew to adulthood.

Another way to look at parts of the complete formal report is to divide them into preliminary, body, and addenda portions as here:

- I. Preliminary parts
  - A. Letter of transmittal
  - B. Title page
  - C. Contents page
  - D. Synopsis or summary (when not in the letter of transmittal)
- II. Body of the report

A. Purpose
B. Method
C. Findings
D. Conclusion/recommendation

III. Addenda

A. Bibliography
B. Appendix
C. Index

This outline includes *all* parts of the complete formal report, but obviously all will not be included in every report. In business, research frequently does not call for bibliography items, reports are usually short enough to eliminate the need for an index, and the transmittal letter often eliminates the need for a summary or synopsis. A brief review of the preliminary and addenda portions is sufficient to provide an understanding of their contents.

The letter of transmittal. Although the letter of transmittal may either precede or follow the title page, the letter is the greeting accompanying the report, as shown in Figure 13–3. It serves the same purpose as would spoken words if the writer were to hand-deliver the report. The writing style is informal, and the transmittal letter takes the following form:

1. Open directly with a statement establishing the subject as in "Here is the report you requested on May 15 about the possibility of using spot radio advertising."

2. Follow the opening with a brief overall review of the report. If a separate summary page will follow, make the review brief. On the other hand, if the letter is to include the summary, it should include the purpose of the report, a brief statement about the method used, highlights of the findings, and a concise conclusion.

3. Close the letter with a look forward to helping again.

The title page. Title pages should include four items: The title, identification of the authority for the report, identification of those who prepared the report, and the date as shown in Figure 13–4. The layout of the title page helps establish the reader's first impression; therefore, special care should be taken in its preparation.

The contents page. Because it reflects the overall report organization and logic, the contents page is an essential part of a long report. This page need not carry the title of the report, and it should be

FIGURE 13–3
Transmittal letter with brief synopsis

June 4, 198_

Mr. Steven C. Miller
Activity Stereo Component Corporation
11689 Santa Monica Boulevard
Beverly Hills, CA 90256

Dear Mr. Miller:

As authorized in your letter of December 6, we conducted a survey of the purchasing preferences of stereo users in the Santa Monica area. We are pleased to submit the attached report to you.

The survey was made by use of a questionnaire distributed to over 3,000 customers of retail stores carrying stereo components.

Over 75 percent of those surveyed either own or plan to purchase stereo systems. Quality was their main concern in stereo systems with power as close second. People under 30 years of age appear to be the prime market group, and they indicated $400 to $600 as the most desirable price range. Based on these and other findings included in the report, we recommend that your advertising program be directed primarily to young adults with stress on quality.

We appreciate the opportunity to assist and are prepared to explore any other area which may be of interest to you.

Sincerely,

Raleigh G. Waller

rgw:ss

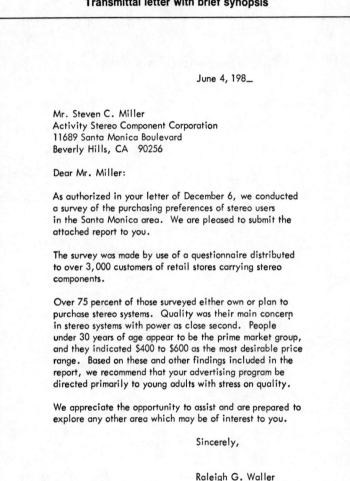

FIGURE 13–4
Title page

THE PURCHASING PREFERENCES OF STEREO USERS

Presented to

Activity Stereo Component Corporation

Prepared by

Slonim-Waller Associates

June 4, 198_

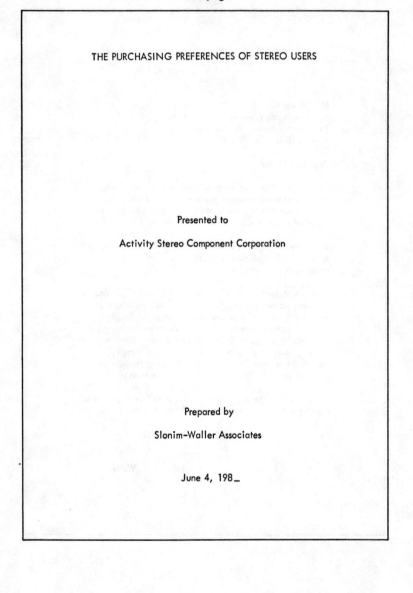

FIGURE 13–5
Contents page

CONTENTS

headed "Contents" or "Table of Contents." All first and second degree headings from the report should be considered minimum for inclusion in the contents, as shown in the sample in Figure 13–5.

The synopsis or summary. For long reports, an opening summary part is desirable. It changes the overall report organization from inductive to deductive. Additionally, it indicates the writer's ability to abstract his own work. Although it may seem repetitious because it capsulizes the report, the summary strengthens communication especially for long or complex reports. Would it be more efficient to read a long report twice or a summary and a long report once?

The addenda. Addenda items contain evidence that lend credibility to reports. A bibliography identifies books, newspapers, periodicals, and other sources used either as findings material or as aids in analyzing the findings. An appendix may contain raw quantitative data, samples of forms or questionnaires, copies of letters, and reproductions of important written items included in the bibliography. An index most frequently is used as an addendum in scholarly publications and textbooks. Although not a part of most reports, an index may be desirable in reports such as internal procedures manuals and personnel handbooks. The final test of whether to include material in the addenda is the writer's judgment of the degree to which the material is necessary to support the body of the report and whether the material might later be called for by a reader.

SUMMARY

The process of organizing reports is pretty much a matter of logical reasoning and knowledge of outlining methods. Once the body of the report is outlined and written, the supporting parts at the beginning and ending of the report are developed. A good report tends to be repetitious simply because the outline indicates the organization and content of the report, and the transmittal letter and synopsis include information that duplicates report content. This duplication is for reader benefit and permits variation in reviewing report content. Repetition is one way of learning.

Chapter 14

USING GRAPHICS IN REPORTS

Although it is probably true that "one picture is worth a thousand words," a picture may be worth many more words than even the thousand. Imagine trying to report in sentence form all the detail available in the single picture represented by a modern financial statement for a major corporation. Or picture the difficulty involved in tying a simple bowline knot from a set of spoken or written instructions without the aid of a demonstration or a picture. Much of the material included in reports is only understandable when written description is accompanied by graphic or tabular aids such as charts, graphs, tables, and pictures.

USING TABLES

The table is a presentation of quantitative data in column form. Very simply, 3 plus 4 plus 12 plus 9 equals 28 is better presented:

$$\begin{array}{r} 3 \\ 4 \\ 12 \\ \underline{9} \\ 28 \end{array}$$

Although the table is not a graphic display in the literal sense of the term *graphic*, it is included in the group of available visual assists because it combines large amounts of data in a concise way. The arrangement of a table is subject to no single guiding principle. Rather, arrangement is a function of the variety and number of items to be included. Several guidelines, however, are appropriate and the application of these guides is illustrated in the sample table shown in Figure 14–1.

1. All tables along with other illustrations in the report should be numbered to provide easy and accurate reference to them in the text.

FIGURE 14–1
Sample table layout

Figure I

Distribution of Stereo System Owners by Occupation

Occupation	Number of Owners	Percent of Owners
White Collar	385	35
Self-employed	271	25
Blue Collar	225	20
Student	153	14
Unemployed	66*	6
Totals	1100	100

*Includes 23 respondents not indicating occupation.

2. Each table should be titled in such a way that the reader understands the content. Therefore, do not economize on words in a title. In the sample, the title might well have been longer to indicate the number of stereo owners surveyed as in: Distribution of 1100 Stereo System Owners by Occupation.
3 Each vertical column of figures and each horizontal line of figures should be captioned. In the sample, the captions or column heads for number and percent of owners could have been arranged in the following way with a common caption and two subcaptions:

Owners	
Number	*Percent*

4. Footnotes should be used to indicate sources—when data were gathered from secondary material—and special instructions. Use asterisks or letters to indicate footnotes. Figures used as indicators may become confused with other figures in the table.
5. Use symbols such as %, #, and $ sparingly in captions. Appropriate style is to spell out words in captions and to use $ before the

first figure in the column of dollar amounts and before the total. Intermediate dollar amounts need no designation.

USING CHARTS

For most business reports, tables are adequate for the presentation of quantitative data. However, when comparative relationships require emphasis, various visual graphic material may be desirable. The following discussion of types of graphics should not be interpreted to mean that any one type is more desirable than others. The types are discussed in random order, and each has obvious desirability depending on the writer's intended purpose for the display.

Pie charts. The pie chart, illustrated in Figure 14–2, provides a dramatic effect when used to show the distribution of parts of a whole. Familiar titles for pie charts are "How Each Dollar of Income Was Distributed," "Distribution of the Average Payroll Dollar," "Percentage Distribution by Countries of World Steel Production," "How Your Tax Dollar Is Used." Picture the pie chart as the face of a clock. The first cut should be made at 12 o'clock; then proceeding clockwise the largest piece of pie should be cut first with the remaining pieces cut in descending order of size. Captions may be placed either within or outside the pie depending on space available, and shadings or color can lend distinction to the various pieces. As a general rule, pie charts should be used only when more than two pieces make up the pie. When two items are being compared, a simple statement should be used in preference to any kind of graphic.

FIGURE 14–2
Pie chart

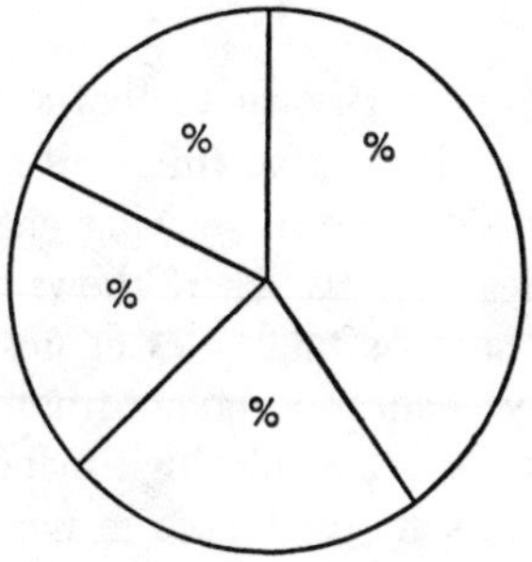

FIGURE 14–3
Bar chart

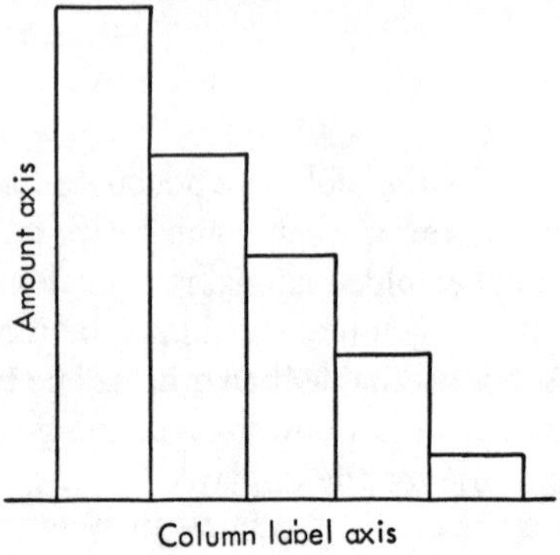

Bar charts. To compare quantities, the bar chart is perhaps the most effective and flexible graphic device. The bar chart is simply a picture of several bars to depict quantities. (See Figure 14–3.) The bars may run either vertically or horizontally. The column label axis may contain labels to indicate years, products, population, or, in fact, almost any line heading found in tables. In essence, the bar chart is a pictorial table.

Good bar chart construction follows these guidelines:

1. When time periods are used for comparison, the periods should run consecutively from earliest to latest on the column label axis. When items other than time periods are used for comparison, place the items of the greatest magnitude on the left with the others proceeding from left to right in order of decreasing magnitude.

2. Bars should be of equal width. Otherwise a short, thick bar may have more mass than a tall thin bar when mass is not the item of comparison.

Line charts. Line charts, similar to that shown in Figure 14–4, are similar to bar charts. Both have time and amount axes, but the line chart is the more desirable in showing changes in quantitative data over time. Whereas the bar chart shows quantitative data for an entire time period such as total sales figures for a year, the line chart is constructed by connecting points from period to period. In this way, the line may show low and high marks for any single unit of time. When line charts are used, keep in mind these guides:

1. Use the vertical axis for amount and the horizontal axis for time.

2. Measure the axis gradations carefully to make certain they are equal. Vertical gradations should be equal, and horizontal gradations should be equal. However, because one axis is time and the other is amount, vertical and horizontal gradations need not be to the same scale.

3. Use reasonable proportions in the size of gradations so the line drawn will be realistic. Dramatic, perhaps unrealistic, lines result from large differences in gradations.

4. Begin both vertical and horizontal axes at 0 on the scale. When the amounts to be shown vertically are so great that the height of

FIGURE 14–4
Line chart

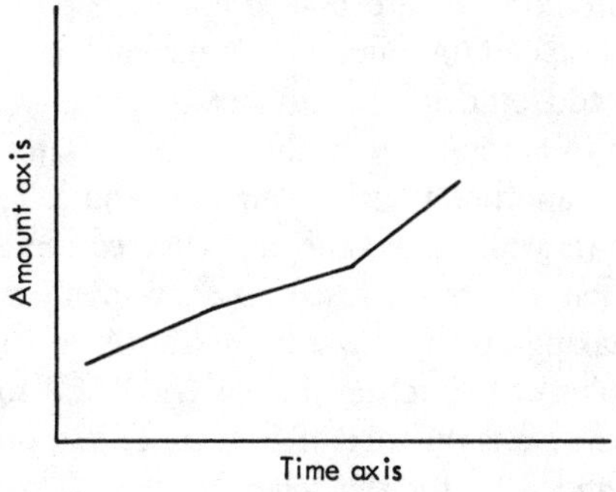

FIGURE 14–5
Broken scale for line chart

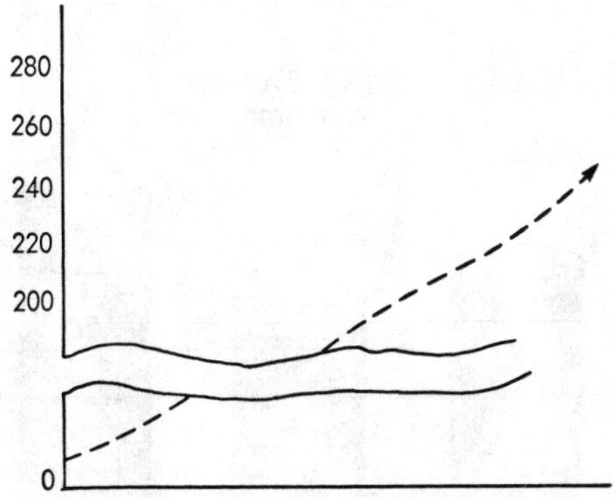

the chart would be unwieldy, break the chart as shown in Figure 14–5. This technique limits the height of the chart without distorting the line.

USING OTHER GRAPHIC TECHNIQUES

Weekly news magazines often dramatize quantitative comparisons through the use of *pictograms* similar to the sample shown in Figure 14–6. Pictures of automobiles, ships, tanks, people, and stacks of dollars are frequently used to assist communication.

The major problem in the use of pictograms is that of maintaining proportions. For example, differences in the quantity of a stack of dollars can be indicated simply by adding or removing dollars. When items such as automobiles are compared, each pictorial automobile should represent a certain number of automobiles. Thus, to show changes, either add or delete a number of pictures. To attempt to show a doubling of automobile production by making one automobile twice as large as another is misleading. As the height of a picture doubles, so does its width. And the area covered increases four times.

Component bar charts are used to show comparisons of wholes and the parts making up those wholes, as shown in Figure 14–7. One bar represents sales of marketing regions (A, B, C) for one year, and the total size of the bar is the total of all sales. The second bar represents sales by region and total for the following year. The component bar chart is similar to a pie chart, then, because the bar represents the division of a whole into its parts, To compare years, however, pie charts would not provide accurate and easy comparison as do component bar charts.

FIGURE 14–6
Pictogram

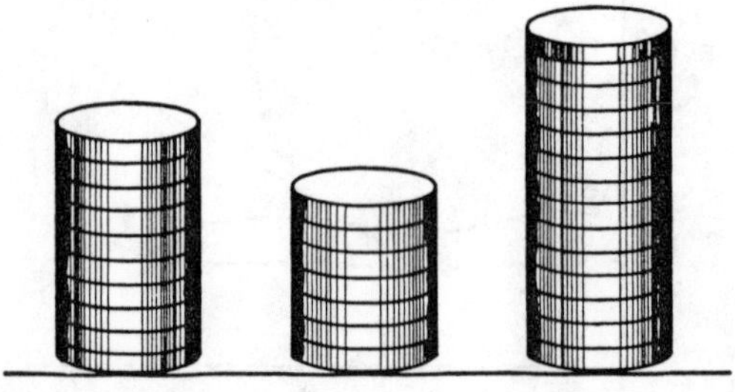

FIGURE 14–7
Component bar chart

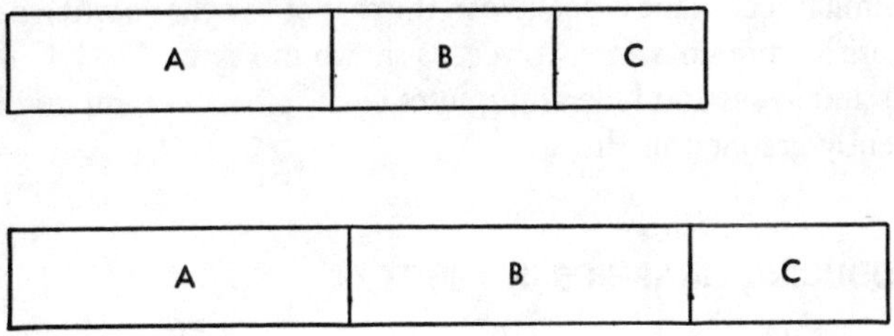

Two techniques are available to accommodate graphic problems when negative amounts are involved. As shown in Figure 14–8, a line chart may be adapted for use when both negative and positive amounts must be shown by simply placing the zero at an intermediate point on the vertical axis. Then, the line may move from positive to negative

FIGURE 14–8
Line chart for negative amounts

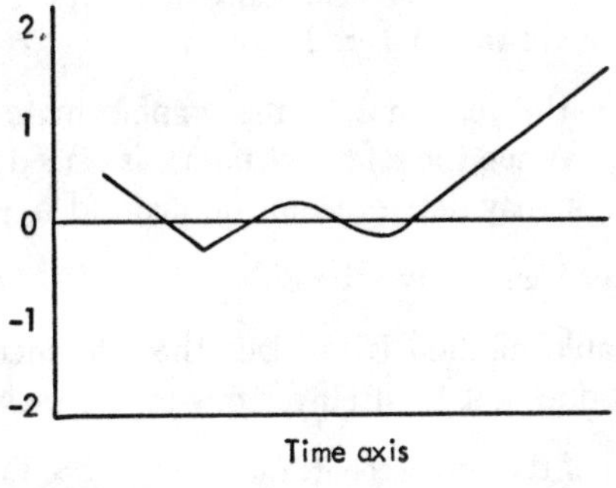

FIGURE 14–9
Bar chart for negative amounts

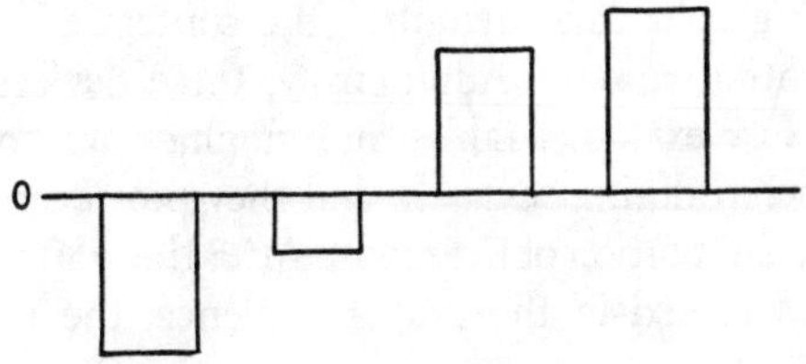

and back and present an accurate picture, for example, of profit figures from year to year.

A similar technique is possible in the case of bar charts when negative and positive amounts are involved, as shown in Figure 14–9. Corporate profits and losses and federal surpluses or deficits are examples of items frequently graphed in this way.

INTRODUCING GRAPHICS IN THE TEXT

A general principle governing use of pictorial or graphic material in reports is that the reader should never come to an illustration unless it has been referred to in the text. Ideally, the material should be introduced before the reader comes to it, and the illustration should be placed as close to its introduction as possible.

Introduction of graphics in the narrative portion of the text can be accomplished in any of several ways. The best method is to use a phrase at the end of a sentence that includes some analysis of the graphic material as follows:

> Two thirds of the new accounts came as the result of our advertising campaign, as shown in Figure 1.

In this example, the reference to the graphic material is incidental to the main idea. When the reference phrase is placed at the beginning of the sentence, it may detract from the main idea, as in:

> As shown in Figure 1, two thirds . . .

The least desirable method is to place the reference in parentheses because it then does not tie itself directly to the main idea.

> Two thirds of the new accounts came . . . . (See Figure 1.)

SUMMARY

Tables and graphs can strengthen the content of reports that are based on quantitative data. Additionally, these devices help ease the writing task. For example, tables and graphics are condensations of raw data gathered during research, and they provide the basis for the narrative (written) portion of the report. After the graphics are prepared, organized, and placed in the proper sequence, the writer need only prepare a written presentation of the analysis and implications of the graphic data.

Therefore, while graphics assist the reader, they also assist the writer by simplifying what might otherwise be a difficult task.

Chapter 15

WRITING THE REPORT

After going through the steps in problem solving, condensing and refining data, and outlining the report, the rest should be easy—all one has to do is put it all in written form. Not surprisingly, most people enjoy doing the field work but dislike the task of writing. A couple of suggestions are appropriate for the insecure writer. First, prepare whatever graphics—tables, pictures, charts—you think you'll need. Writing is much easier when you can see what you are writing about. Second, use the outline as a tentative guide, because you can always make minor changes. Then, begin your writing with any item in the outline. Start with the thing you are most familiar with even if it might be the conclusions or recommendations which will ultimately appear at the end of the report. In other words, proceed from the familiar to the unfamiliar—from those things you feel secure about to those things less secure in your mind.

USING IMPERSONAL STYLE

One of the striking things about report-writing problems is the difficulty writers often have in writing naturally. Because they have become accustomed to writing in first-person style and using personal pronouns such as *you* and *I*, writers fail to achieve the degree of objectivity they think a report should profess. We seem to operate under the idea that reports should eliminate pronouns completely and appear so antiseptic that humans had nothing to do with them. Such need not be the case. The personal pronoun can be eliminated and the report can still be natural and unstilted.

Sentences beginning "It is believed . . ." or "It is submitted . . ." leave the reader confused about the subject *It.* In informal report writing style, "I believe . . ." is quite appropriate. As the report approaches the formal end of the continuum, however, personal pronouns become undesirable. You can develop skill in avoiding the personal pronouns while still writing interesting and natural messages. Recasting sentences is a skill all good report writers develop. Note the following sentences which all say the same thing:

> *Using the pronoun:* I distributed questionnaires to 300 workers.
>
> *Recasting the sentence:* Questionnaires were distributed to 300 workers; or Distribution of questionnaires was made to 300 workers; or Three hundred workers completed questionnaires.

In the example using the pronoun *I,* some writers would eliminate *I* by saying "The author distributed questionnaires. . . ." This technique leads to great awkwardness and may be a lie if taken literally. The important thing to remember is that you can recast a sentence in several ways.

The pronoun *you* tends to increase interest, because it brings the reader into the story. However, *you* also tends to be persuasive and may decrease the desired objectivity. In introductory remarks such as "You will notice the contrast between . . . ," the *you* can be avoided and action improved by simply saying "Notice the contrast between. . . ."

Company practices vary in the degree of formality in reports and in the use of personal pronouns. A little practice will enable you to adopt effective impersonal style when necessary.

USING ACTIVE SENTENCES

Because reporting usually involves writing about some kind of action, active writing is often appropriate. In the following example, passive voice is converted to active by recasting the sentence:

> *Passive:* The contract was reviewed thoroughly by the attorney.
>
> *Active:* The attorney thoroughly reviewed the contract.

In the passive example, the subject *contract* did nothing—took no action. In the active example, the subject *attorney* took some action—

reviewed the contract. In active voice, the subject is the doer of the action. In passive voice, the subject is the receiver of the action. The writer must decide whether active or passive should be used to emphasize the proper elements. In the example above, *contract* receives emphasis in the passive sentence and *attorney* in the active sentence, because the subject of the sentence is always the key part.

Passive sentences always use some form of the verb *to be* such as *is, was, have been,* and *are.* To attempt to eliminate them would be foolish. However, should you find that all your sentences have passive verbs, you should attempt to achieve balance. About one active sentence out of every four or five is adequate to maintain this balance. You will recall from earlier chapters the discussion of sentence organization and ways to vary it. The emphasis given here is to use the techniques in achieving an objective report-writing style.

USING PROPER TENSE

Anyone who has read many master's or doctor's degree theses is aware that passive voice coupled with past tense verbs leads to deadly reading. To avoid this problem, simply keep in mind that anything done before writing the report is reported in past tense. You *developed* a plan of attack, you *gathered* data, and you *reached* a conclusion. As you direct the reader through the report, you *call* attention to a table that *shows* information. You may remind the reader that a preceding chapter *showed* something. In other words, write about things as they occur, and you should have few problems.

USING ACCURATE NOUNS AND PRONOUNS

An abundance of references such as *it, those, their, these,* and *aforementioned* will help lose the reader quickly. Sooner or later the reader will look for an antecedent and find none, two, or singular and plural. Because a pronoun is a word that stands for a noun, it should not stand for a sentence, a paragraph, or an idea. When in doubt, repeat the noun rather than attempt to get by with a nebulous pronoun. For example, when you are tempted to write: "Procedures have been modified. These account for the delay," simply repeat the noun by saying "Procedures have been modified. These modifications account for the delay." In the first example, "These" may refer to either the procedures or the modifications. In the second, the meaning is definite. Fix your meaning.

USING COMMON LANGUAGE

Because most reports contain discussion of some form of quantitative data, some language should be used to make complicated data understandable to a variety of readers. Take, for example, a report to stockholders saying sales for the current year were $77,985,676 and for the previous year amounted to $62,432,771. Very few can visualize amounts of those sizes, nor can many rapidly calculate the increase of some $15.5 million. Most people do understand percentages and ratios. We could say sales increased $15.5 million or 20 percent. We could even write that for every $4 of sales last year we had $5 in sales this year.

Common language use enables the writer to reduce large amounts to understandable terms. The place for common language is in the written analysis of data shown in tables and other graphic presentations. Common language in the narrative report is a written description of the meaning one gathers when reviewing a graphic presentation.

Symbols such as $, %, ¢, and # are part of our common language. Almost everyone understands the meaning of certain symbols. Within an industry, "jargon"—the language of the trade—becomes common language. To use jargon when communicating with people outside the industry, however, is to ensure poor communication.

Economic changes make the dollar a shaky common language for comparative purposes, too. Manufacturing industries speak in terms of units: automobiles produced, freight car loadings, passenger miles. Report writing is at its communicative best when difficult-to-understand concepts and figures are reduced to concise, common-language statements.

USING TABULATIONS

Frequently listing several items is necessary in reports. Notice the difference between the following paragraphs:

> Therefore, the Hi-Bubble Cola eight-bottle package should be converted to a six-bottle package because of a lower shelf price, a competitive price with other packages, easier handling by consumers, and an appearance conducive to single-bottle sales.

The improved version:

Therefore, the Hi-Bubble Cola eight-bottle package should be converted to a six-bottle package for the following reasons:

1. A lower shelf price.
2. A competitive price with other packages.
3. Easier handling by consumers.
4. An appearance conducive to single-bottle sales.

The improved version uses tabulations and enumeration to emphasize the four reasons for the recommendation. The lead-in statement for the revised version could also have used the phrase "because of" as a substitute for "for the following reasons." However, the lead-in phrasing preceding tabulations represents one of the difficult areas in reporting writing. If each tabulated item does not read easily with "because of," an awkward series results. Such awkwardness can detract from the reader's understanding of the statements. To check parallel construction in a tabulated statement, read each item separately with the lead-in phrasing.

USING DEFINITIONS

Frequently a writer feels an obligation to define terms used in the report. Definitions are rather easy to construct when the concept of dividing and classifying discussed in Chapter 13 is kept in mind. The process of outlining contributes to the elements in a good definition.

Three elements are included in definitions: (1) The term to be defined, (2) the family to which the term belongs, and (3) the differentiation that makes the term different from all other members of the family. In the outline of the United States used in Chapter 13, Massachusetts was classified as a Northeastern state. To write a definition of Massachusetts, then, using the three elements, we have:

The term: *Massachusetts.*
The family: *United States.*
The differentiation: *Northeastern.*

Thus, Massachusetts is one of the United States and is located in the Northeast. The basic definition could then be embellished with further distinguishing characteristics: Massachusetts is one of the fifty United States and is located in the Northeast bordered by Vermont and New Hampshire on the north and Connecticut and Rhode Island on the south.

as paragraphs in a composition must be related, so must sections of a report. Here are some of the acceptable devices.

Repetition of words. Notice how the transition from one paragraph to the next occurs in the following example despite an intervening heading.

> . . . and lengthy sentences are deterrents to understanding in reports.
>
> *Difficult Wording*
>
> Although lengthy sentences are deterrents, difficult wording . . .

Repetition of an idea. In the above example, repetition of words led to transition. Notice how the following sentences are tied together by repeating the idea but not the exact words.

> . . . as a result of the practice of polygamy. On the other hand, plural marriages . . .

Reference to something to come. A statement at the end of one section similar to the following will ensure transition:

> In the following section, attention will be focused on . . .

Use of transitional words or phrases. Here are some examples of transitional words or phrases that can be of help when other devices seem difficult to incorporate:

Time transitions	*Contrast and similarity transitions*
further	similarly
furthermore	in the same way
next	the same
for example	likewise
for instance	however
in other words	on the other hand
specifically	on the contrary
meanwhile	nevertheless
the latter	but
as mentioned	yet
then	while
as suggested	in contrast
in the first place	although
in the second place	in a different vein
finally	despite

Other helpful words and phrases

therefore	in conclusion
in summary	not only
as a result	moreover
since	provided
because	consequently
at the same time	briefly
hence	conversely
thus	

SUMMARY

Although the style of writing used in reports is far more formal than the natural, conversational style used in letters, report writers can develop a natural formal style. The art of recasting sentences to avoid personal pronouns and still retain action and interest can be developed by following some of the suggestions in this chapter. In addition to achieving a tone of objectivity through writing style, writers can add credibility to their reports by applying appropriate mechanical and expository techniques discussed in the next chapter.

Chapter 16

FINISHING THE REPORT

Previous chapters have dealt with the report process, research, outlining, use of graphics, and writing style. Before putting the report in its final form, the writer should keep in mind several factors which contribute to the finished product.

USING OBJECTIVITY

Writing effectively involves the intelligent use of statements that explain or reveal the analysis that went into the development of the topic. When decisions are to be made by management, the report should be objective enough to permit decisions to be free of the subjective opinion or biases of the writer. Objective writing is characterized by (a) avoidance of emotional terms, (b) recognition of assumptions and opinions, and (c) use of only requested judgments and inferences.

Emotional terms are words or phrases which are persuasive in meaning and which generally cannot be supported by research data. Such words as *shocking, startling,* and *amazing* should not be used in discussions of research findings in reports. In oral presentations such terms may be used as spontaneous comments. But with the amount of thought that goes into problem solving and report preparation, such terms only detract from the presentation. What is amazing to one person may be only humdrum to another. Let readers make their own emotional appraisals.

Assumptions are an important part of most research. When sampling is used for surveys, we make the assumption that the sample of the population surveyed is representative of the population. If the assumption is that the findings should be related only to the group surveyed and not to a larger population, the reader should be told about it. Therefore, review your research carefully to make sure all your assumptions are apparent. Put them in the report; otherwise, the reader may not arrive at the same conclusion you did.

Opinions are often easier to recognize than assumptions. An opinion is a conclusion or inference about something but falls short of positive knowledge. The doctor, dentist, accountant, real estate appraiser, and other professionals often give opinions which, in the absence of positive knowledge, are considered the nearest thing to fact. When you are inclined to include an opinion in the report, give the reader the privilege of being informed. Simply say "In my opinion" or "In the opinion of counsel."

A *judgment* is the writer's opinion about the good or bad of something. Smoking may be detrimental to health. Excess fat in the diet may contribute to heart disease. Such statements as these are the results of research. But notice how the wording stays within the findings of research because not all people who smoke and eat fat suffer from those activities. However, most of us have drawn our own judgments about the good or bad of such activities. Judgments in reports should be avoided unless they have been requested.

Judgment implies decision making and, thus, touches on a very sensitive area of business. The right and responsibility of making decisions is inherent in the lines of authority and responsibility of the organization structure. The good report writer reviews the authority given for the report. Was a recommendation requested? Or were findings and conclusions all that were necessary? Don't go beyond the purpose of the study.

An *inference* is a close relative of a judgment. Inferences are statements about the unknown based on the known. Because we can't see into the future with great accuracy, any statement about the future lies in the area of an inference. At the same time, business relies heavily on its ability to predict the future. It attempts to gather as much evidence as possible, analyze it from many viewpoints, and make predictions with an accuracy far better than chance. The same admonition applies to inferences, then, as apply to the other terms discussed. Stay within the confines of the problem. If an inference is called for, give it—but also recognize it for what it is.

"Weasel" words are frequently used by good writers to reveal the degree to which they are willing to stand behind their findings. Such words as *indicate, suggest, point, show,* and *hint* are helpful. When data do not prove a point, they often suggest or indicate possible conclusions. Statements such as "The data indicate a potential consumer move in . . ." may be far more objective than "A consumer move in . . ." simply because the data do not indicate a certainty. Although no hierarchy of strength or objectivity exists for the use of weasel words, a possible strength sequence might be *show, indicate, point, suggest,* and *hint.* Coupling any of these with such terms as *possibility* or *potential* may further modify the degree to which the writer wants to "stick out his neck." At any rate, "weasel" words should be used cautiously.

USING DOCUMENTATION

Documentation in a report is accomplished in several ways. Essentially, documentation is the process of "giving credit where credit is due." Using footnotes, bibliographies, and textual references to sources are generally accepted methods of documentation. Although these methods may assist the reader, they serve the writer in many more ways:

1. Protect the writer against plagiarism. In general practice, quoted or paraphrased material of two or three lines may be referenced by a footnote without requesting permission. When material is to be circulated widely, as in a text or article, and is also sizable, permission should be sought from the original source. Government publications may be quoted freely, however.
2. Protect the writer's professional integrity. In other words, don't quote excerpts from the work of others and claim it as your own.
3. Support the writer's statements. If recognized authorities say the same thing you do, your work takes on reliability. Documentation enables your work to be verified.

Using footnotes. Footnotes shown at the bottom of the page are referred to by citation numbers in the text as in this example.[1]

> [1] William C. Himstreet and Wayne Murlin Baty, *Business Communications,* 6th ed. (Boston: Kent Publishing Company, 1981), p. 370.

In academic work, the bottom-of-the-page footnote is most used. In business reports, a faster and simpler method is the terminal reference. All sources are listed in the bibliography in alphabetical order and each is given a number. In the text, a notation such as (4:16) is made immediately following the material to be cited. In this example, (4:16), the 4 refers to the fourth item in the bibliography, and the 16 refers to the page number from which the material was taken.

In the sample footnote, notice that the author's given name came first. This same entry shown in a bibliography would have the surname first.

Footnote entries may also be used to explain formulas, document interviews or other sources of unwritten information, and for information this is difficult to incorporate in the text.

Preparing bibliographies. Bibliography entries differ in two respects from footnotes. First, bibliography entries refer to the entire work cited rather than to specific pages. Second, as noted previously, given names come first in footnotes, and surnames come first in bibliography entries. Author "John Doe" in a footnote becomes "Doe, John" in a bibliography. All literature appearing as footnotes also appears in the bibliography. Here are some suggestions for handling bibliography items:

1. When only a few items will appear, simply list them all—books, periodicals, government reports—in alphabetical sequence. If large bibliographies, say of several pages, are to be used, group them by categories.

2. Government publications are listed under "U.S. Department of . . ." in the bibliography with the departments followed by the title determining the alphabetical sequence. In footnotes, the title of the publication comes first.

3. Your primary concern in a bibliography is to tell your reader what you've used and where to find it. Such things as newspaper items and annual reports may well be included.

Here are some forms of proper bibliography entries:

For a book:

> Horton, Paul B., and Robert L. Horton. *Programmed Learning Aid for Introductory Sociology*. Homewood, Ill.: Learning Systems Company, 1971. 137 pages.

For an article:

> Day, Martin L. "Say It Right." *Language Journal*, vol. 19, no. 3 (May 1974). P. 101.

For a government publication:

> U.S. Department of Agriculture. Forest Service. *Dry Farming Possibilities for Guayule in California*. Washington, D.C.: U.S. Government Printing Office, 1946.

Using textual references. Frequently, statements can be supported by parenthetical references to sources. For example, "According to a recent commitment by the Board of Directors, the company will issue discount coupons to . . ." is a statement preceded by the phrase documenting the authority for the statement. The same thing would apply in the following: "In a speech to the Commonwealth Club last week, Secretary Hooper gave support to. . . ." In such cases, footnotes or bibliography references are unnecessary.

WRITING PARTS OF THE REPORT BODY

The following suggestions are intended to ease the task of beginning each part of the report body.

Writing the introduction. The introduction of a report, whether it be a memorandum or a long formal presentation, should include as a minimum a statement of purpose and a description of the method used. In longer reports, many writers like to end the introduction with a brief statement of the organization of the remainder of the body. Therefore, an outline of the introductory section which begins on the first page of the body would appear as follows:

Introduction
- Purpose
- Method(s) used
- Organization of the report

Normally, a report should not have two consecutive headings without intervening writing. Therefore, the heading "Introduction" should have some remarks following it before the subheading "Purpose" appears, as shown in Figure 16–1, a sample introductory page. The material following the introductory heading may simply establish the importance of the subject studied or it may go to great lengths to provide background for the study.

The easiest way to state the purpose of the study is to begin with "The purpose of this study was to analyze . . ." or "The purpose of this report is to present an analysis of. . . ." As you write this section, remember that "studies analyze" and "reports present." Reports can't analyze, but people can.

Following a heading for method, the first few words may well be "To gather data, a questionnaire survey was conducted. . . ." Within the method section, list sources of information. How many people were surveyed? What was the population? If sampling were used, why is it reliable?

If a section on organization of the report is to be used, a statement such as the following is appropriate: "Following parts of the report present in order the cost, size, power, and comfort analyses of the three aircraft. The final section contains conclusions and recommendations."

As mentioned in Chapter 13, the headings "introduction," "purpose," "methods," and others used in the introductory section of a report may be omitted because readers expect the initial part of a report to be an introduction. Compare the first page shown in Figure 16–1 to the first page in Figure 16–2 that omits the introductory headings. In this second version, the title of the report is generally placed at the top of the page.

Writing about the findings. As the report leaves the introductory portions and enters the findings, a first degree heading should appear. A major weakness of reports is that they often rely on headings for thought. Actually, a report should stand by itself without the use of headings. In other words, if all headings were removed, would the report still be understandable? For example:

> *Cost Favors the Bobcat*
> This factor was studied by gathering data from all three manufacturers and comparing. . . .

Note that the sentence following the heading would not make sense if the heading were removed, because "This factor . . ." relied on the heading for sense. If the sentence began "The cost factor . . . ," then the sentence is understandable even without the heading. Don't hesitate to establish the proper subject even if it is repetitious of the heading.

When tables are involved, language such as "Table I shows the comparative cost factors" is really wasted because the title of the table says the same thing. Improved language would be similar to the following: "The Bobcat has a 12 percent cost advantage, as shown in Table I." Make each sentence in the findings sections say something about the analysis of data.

As a final word about presenting findings, review the material about transition in Chapter 15. Attention to transition from section to section

FIGURE 16–1
Sample first page

INTRODUCTION

Television news broadcasting is one of the most competitive branches of the broadcasting industry. Time of day, format, and personalities are competitive elements that lead to viewer popularity.

Purpose of the Study

The purposes of this study were to determine the following information: (1) the viewer popularity ratings of personalities on local, non-national, television newscasts, and (2) the influence of other factors leading to viewer popularity. Channel 8 plans to use the results of this study to assess its status in the news field.

Method and Sources

To obtain data for the study, a questionnaire survey was conducted by mail to 1,200 selected persons. The population surveyed was within range of Channel 8 and its competitors. Individuals were selected on geographic, economic, occupation, and sex bases. Of the 1,200 questionnaires mailed, 934 were returned and deemed usable. A copy of the questionnaire and transmittal letter are included in Appendix A, page 27.

Organization of the Report

The remainder of this report presents in sequence an analysis of the popularity of anchormen, analysts, sports

FIGURE 16–2
Sample first page without headings

STATUS OF CHANNEL 8 IN NEWS BROADCASTING — 1981

Television news broadcasting is one of the most competitive branches of the broadcasting industry. Time of day, format, and personalities are competitive elements that lead to viewer popularity.

The purposes of this study were to determine the following information: (1) the viewer popularity ratings of personalities on local, non-national, television, newscasts, and (2) the influence of other factors leading to viewer popularity. Channel 8 plans to use the results of this study to assess its status in the news field.

To obtain data for the study, a questionnaire survey was conducted by mail to 1,200 selected persons. The population surveyed was within range of Channel 8 and its competitors. Individuals were selected on geographic, economic, occupation, and sex bases. Of the 1,200 questionnaires mailed, 934 were returned and deemed usable. A copy of the questionnaire and transmittal letter are included in Appendix A, page 27.

The remainder of this report presents in sequence an analysis of the popularity of anchormen, analysts, sports

1

will make the report coherent and assure smoothness for the reader.

Writing about conclusions and recommendations. The conclusions arrived at are generalizations about the findings. Therefore, a statement beginning with "Based on the findings, the following conclusions were . . ." provides an appropriate lead-in to a presentation of one or more conclusions.

Recommendations grow out of conclusions and should appropriately follow them. In some reports, a recommendation is placed immediately following the conclusion on which it is based. In others, all conclusions are presented, and then all recommendations are presented as a group.

SUMMARY

Finishing the report should be a satisfying job—it marks the culmination of a major effort. Yet, writing the final draft is often a painstaking, almost unbearable chore for most writers. It needn't be so when writers understand the report process and can visualize how the final product will look. Because the report consists of rather distinct parts, begin writing with the part that seems most familiar. The pieces can then be put together using transitional techniques. Above all, write rapidly; and set aside large enough time blocks for writing that you can accomplish something. Rapid writing of the rough draft enables you to keep up with your thought processes, and the long writing period permits you to do more than simply get your mind "warmed up." Do not do any editing until you have a complete rough draft prepared. Then, set the draft aside for a while before you attempt to edit for final typing. These guides for writing carry an implication that the good report writer establishes a time schedule for the process. Work your schedule back from the due date of the report so you have time to work comfortably. Last-minute rush crises will almost always have a negative effect on report quality.

Chapter 17

PREPARING MEMORANDUMS AND SHORT REPORTS

A century ago, American industry was characterized by small businesses. One- and two-person businesses were the rule rather than the exception, and internal communication was simple. The proximity of management and employees was conducive to two-way, face-to-face communication. As a matter of fact, few typewriters existed so written communication was pretty well limited to hand-written letters or mass mailings of printed material. With the growth of large businesses, however, management developed an increasing need for a flow of information not available through oral means. Thus, the internal memorandum and short report became the primary tools of non-oral communication.

CHARACTERISTICS OF INTERNAL REPORTS

The memorandum is the most-used report is business. Perhaps the best distinction between a memorandum and a short report is that the short report is longer than a memorandum. At the same time, memorandums flow upward, downward, and laterally in organizations. Short reports tend to flow upward as a rule. Thus, some characteristics of reports are that they

1. Flow upward because most reports are requested by a higher authority in the organization.
2. Stress objectivity through the writer's attention to planning and physical layout.
3. Are usually written for a small readership—often only one person.
4. Follow the problem-solving steps.
5. Contribute to the management decision making process.

Memorandums, as distinguished from reports, flow in various directions, may incorporate letter-planning style to anticipate reader reaction, and do not necessarily require much attention to planning and physical layout. Therefore, writers must use their good judgment to determine when the message content should be prepared as a simple memorandum and when it should take on some of the planning and layout characteristics of reports. The subject, the needs of the reader, the complexity of the material, and the ultimate use of the message are criteria to be considered.

WRITING METHODS

The primary purpose of memorandums is to contribute to clear organizational communication. Very simply, when people know what is going on and how they fit into the total picture, their performance generally is improved. To play its role, the memorandum incorporates qualities from letters as well as from reports.

In writing style and tone, the memorandum is similar to letters. In overall organization and presentation methods, it takes qualities from formal reports. In any case, the memorandum assumes, as suggested earlier, a plan of presentation and a degree of formality based on ultimate use, reader needs, and complexity of material.

A format feature of the memorandum, as well as the short report, is the to-from-subject-date heading shown in Figure 17–1. In most firms, memorandums follow a consistent format which provides control over accuracy by placing all items in the same position each time. This is often assured by using printed forms.

The sample memorandum in Figure 17–1 incorporates several helpful guides for writers:

1. Use the subject line for two purposes: *(a)* To assist the reader by making the subject clear, and *(b)* to assist the writer forcing him or her to develop a clear understanding of the problem. If a person cannot prepare an appropriate subject line, how can he or she write effectively about the subject?
2. Use the first sentence to restate the subject. The content of a message should not rely on the subject line, or other headings, for thought. References such as "the above subject," "the aforementioned subject," and "this subject" should be avoided. Write the body of the memorandum as though the subject line did not exist. In this way, you prepare the body of the report as a complete composition; and you hit the reader with a repetition of the major

FIGURE 17–1
Memorandum report

To: Arnold Tucker   Date: February 7, 198_

From: M.W. Welds

Subject: Future of the Ontario Speedway

I have completed the analysis of scheduling and operating problems of the Ontario Speedway as you requested. Schedules were reviewed, information gathered on the present financial condition of the speedway was analyzed, and an attempt was made to estimate future possibilities.

1982 Schedule

The 1982 schedule does not include any additional major events. It is unlikely that additional racing events can be scheduled at this late date.

Outdoor concerts are a big financial risk, and it is doubtful whether any of the tentative or scheduled concerts will in reality become a major event.

Financial Position

As explained in the attached clipping from the Los Angeles Times of January 10, the California 500 race on March 9 may determine the future of the present management of the speedway. The present group may default on their lease after the 500. From my information, the advance sales are not keeping pace with those of previous years.

Future Possibilities

If the present leaseholders default, the speedway will probably be closed for only a short time. Because of the investment of the bond holders and the obligations of the City of Ontario, every effort will be made to negotiate an operating agreement with a new group.

Recommendations

1. Arrange a meeting as soon as possible with the present management to discuss the future of the Hi-Bubble California Grand Prix.

2. Prepare alternate plans for promotion if we cannot sponsor the Grand Prix.

purpose, even though you do not use the identical words. Advertising provides evidence that repetition is an effective way of communicating.

3. Use the introductory paragraph as an introduction to the report. In the sample memorandum, the first paragraph includes both the purpose and the methods used to achieve the purpose just as does the introductory portion of a formal report.
4. Use subheadings when desirable to indicate organization and to separate distinct topics.

Each of these guides is also applicable to formal reports. In the case of the sample, it could be described as a short report because of the incorporation of these guiding suggestions. Also note that the sample is organized in inductive or indirect sequence by proceeding through the problem solving steps to arrive at conclusions and recommendations. Ordinarily, however, the deductive sequence is desirable for informational reports. In a deductively organized report, the first paragraph would serve as a total summary and would include the conclusion as would the summary at the beginning of a formal report.

SUMMARY

The distinction between memorandums and short reports is a fine one. "Drop into my office, Joe, on your next trip west. I'd like your views on restructuring the marketing staff" could be the content of a simple memorandum. On the other hand, the memorandum could take the form of the sample used in this chapter and, thus, be described as a short report. The simple memorandum could be written in longhand without much preplanning. The short report would probably call for a rough draft to be reviewed before final typing.

When you have prepared a rough draft, make the necessary adjustments for final typing. Then read the entire draft aloud to yourself and do some editing. Reading the report aloud is a revealing practice. It reveals all the awkward wording, lack of coherence, and gaps in logic. Silent reading doesn't achieve the same ends. Finally, give the finished typing job a "once over" to assure yourself of its overall quality. Much faulty communication occurs when we place too much trust in the typist.

Chapter 18

LISTENING AND MAKING ORAL PRESENTATIONS

In this chapter, you'll study listening, first as a basis for developing skill in making oral presentations.

Study after study on how adults spend their time have shown that communication occupies us about three fourths of our awake hours. We spend 45 minutes of every awake hour either reading, speaking, writing, or listening. Although only ten or fifteen percent of our communicative time is spent writing, writing is a communicative skill operating at the one-way, or least effective, communication level. At the other extreme, timewise, is listening—a skill occupying about half of all our communicative time. The purpose of this chapter is to review methods of improving the active, two-way skill involved in oral communication—listening and speaking.

Perhaps the greatest key to effective face-to-face communication is the listener's willingness, followed by his ability, to listen. We all probably speak well enough to be understood if we know what we want to say. On the other hand, we all have the listening equipment—eyes, minds, and ears—to listen for understanding. Often, though, we find ourselves and others simply hearing and not listening.

If you can recall the schematic presentation of the communication process shown in Chapter 1, the destination of a message is the mind of the receiver. And the mind is an extremely active place. Unchallenged it creates its own challenges. When listening is going on, the mind has a tendency to do other things—daydream, solve problems, develop messages for us to send, and, in general, keep busy doing things that turn our listening process into one of hearing only. Hearing is a physical process. It picks up sounds. Listening is both a physical and a mental process.

DETRIMENTAL LISTENING HABITS

Really good listeners are rare. They have the ability to block out all distractions and focus eyes, ears, and minds on the sounds coming to them. Poor listeners, or average ones for that matter, have developed one or more bad listening habits that plague human communication. Good speakers can hold a listener's attention for long periods, it's true; but not enough of the messages coming to us are delivered by fascinating platform speakers.

As we listen to someone talking, we are accepting messages being delivered at about 125 to 150 words a minute on the average. Unfortunately, we have the ability to read two to ten times that fast. And our minds operate at thousands of words a minute in terms of thought. Therefore, the listener's mental equipment is moving at many times the rate of the message. The mind has lots of spare time to do other things unless it is disciplined. As a result of these differences in speed and of our own ego involvement—concern for our own affairs—we have developed habits detrimental to good listening. Let's review some of these detrimental habits.

First, we are fakers of attention. Haven't you had the experience of listening—or supposedly listening—to someone only to discover later that you have no idea what was said. In the office, the club, the home? You look at the speaker, smile with him, nod assent, even lean forward wide-eyed. But you are faking. You fake the speaker into thinking you are listening. Hopefully, from your point of view, you won't have to provide sensible feedback, because you can't.

Second, we criticize delivery and physical appearance. If the speaker doesn't come up to our standards of what makes a good speaker or of what constitutes a satisfactory physical appearance, we turn off our listening equipment just as though it were controlled by an electric on-off switch. Even little things have the capacity to turn us off. A mole on a cheek, unusual dress, awkward gestures, and even unshined shoes are things that can capture attention to the point of disrupting listening.

Third, we listen to what we want to listen to. We can rationalize poor listening by claiming the subject was uninteresting. Therefore, we treat subjects just as we do speakers; we blame them for our listening failures.

A fourth bad habit is over-listening. This occurs usually when we are determined not to miss a word of a lecture or speech. As the speaker proceeds through the presentation, we try to remember every detail, every statistic, every anecdote. We are so busy fixing these in our minds that when major points are made, we aren't listening because our minds are occupied with the task of recording the minor items used to support the major points. The good listener knows the structure of a speech, which we'll come to later in this chapter.

Last, of course, we develop laziness. We avoid listening to something that may appear too difficult. We can blame modern technology for this. Television provides us with several options. If a program is too difficult, we can change channels to search for something less challenging.

Because listening is obviously a responsibility of the listener, we can't blame speakers. The task of channeling our entire receiving apparatus on a message requires significant discipline, both mental and physical. Let's review some suggestions for developing this discipline.

EFFECTIVE LISTENING SUGGESTIONS

Perhaps the primary suggestion for improving listening is. "take the time to listen." In our face-to-face communication activities such as conversing and interviewing, we have a tendency to spend much time formulating in our own minds what we are going to say when it's our turn to talk. Often this is done at the expense of effective listening. Carl Rogers, an advocate of the nondirective counseling technique, has said that therapeutic counseling should take the form of listening more than of talking. Given an opportunity to talk about their problems, people will resolve them for themselves most of the time. And many times when people think they have problems, the opportunity to talk about them will reveal that they had no problem at all. They simply wanted to "get something off their chests."

People have a primary need to be heard, to be appreciated, to be wanted. By taking the time to listen, a person can satisfy the other person's need. Aren't many of your own best friends also good listeners? Therefore, good listening can be classed as a valuable social grace as well as an asset in our business lives.

The office desk is a barrier to effective listening, because it not only separates the speaker and the listener, but it also holds papers and other distracting items. Nothing is more distracting to a visitor than for the person on the other side of the desk to attempt to read items on the desk during the discussion. Of course, nothing is more disconcerting to the host than to have the visitor also attempt to read mail on the desk—even upside down. Therefore, for effective office interviewing, try to eliminate the desk as a barrier. If side chairs are available, retreat to those. You'll be surprised how much more effective the communications and how much faster the interview goes.

When listening to a speech or lecture, of course, you don't have the privilege of providing oral feedback to the speaker or of eliminating barriers such as the desk. As a result, you are on your own to get as much from the speech as possible. As with any other kind of effective listening, try these suggestions.

1. Watch the speaker. We listen as much with our eyes as with our ears. The nonverbal aids to communication such as facial expressions and arm gestures add much to the spoken word. You can detect when the speaker is deadly serious, casual, or humorous.
2. Listen between the lines. Frequently, through a combination of words and nonverbal aids, the listener can identify meanings not apparent in the words alone. In addition, a series of statements may imply something not apparent in any of the statements taken individually.
3. Think along with the speaker, then attempt to anticipate what the presentation is leading to and what conclusions will be drawn. In this way, the good listener has his mind tuned in to the presentation. He can weigh the evidence presented in terms of his own logic, detect weaknesses in arguments, and, in general, separate small talk from major points.
4. Occasionally, review the organization of the presentation in your own mind. You might even be able to construct a mental outline of the talk after a little practice.

As you study the remainder of this chapter on making oral reports, keep the listening discussion in mind. The better you understand the habits, good and bad, of your audience, the better you are able to adapt your oral presentations.

We all remember a dynamic speaker we heard at one time. But how many of us remember the topic after only a short time. Public speaking, for most professional speakers, is really an act—half is content and half is showmanship. The typical business person is not a professional speaker. Nevertheless, business people must from time to time appear before colleagues, professional societies, civic organizations, and other groups. As they move up the ladder in their organizations, people will definitely have to make oral presentations before members of their own organizations. The speaking roles we'll discuss are those described as public speaking and as oral reporting. Public speaking occurs outside the firm; oral reporting is part of the firm's internal communication process and occurs between the reporter and his or her colleagues.

In either case, speakers will use one of four styles: impromptu, extemporaneous, memorized, or written-and-read. The *impromptu* speech occurs when the speaker is called on to speak but has no forewarning. This can be a frightening experience for beginners. *Extemporaneous* speaking is done with the use of a few notes, but it is a style that most good speakers use. They know in advance that they will speak and are able to prepare and practice. By being familiar with their material and using few notes, they are able to benefit from and adapt to audience reaction. *Memorized* speeches are familiar to all of us through our experiences in school, church, and organizations. Memorizing has limitations. The speaker is unable to adjust to audience feedback, temporary memory blocks are embarrassing, and speaker body motions appear to be unnatural. The *written-and-read* speaking style is appropriate for many technical or complex presentations. Again, the speaker has difficulty adjusting to the audience and is often stuck so tightly to the speech manuscript that he or she fails to make eye contact with the audience.

As you review these four types, you should agree that the extemporaneous style is something to work toward. Your first efforts may consist almost entirely of written-and-read talks; then as you gain confidence, you can move into the extemporaneous style. If you write your speech, follow these guides:

1. Write your notes large enough so that you can easily read them, and leave wide spaces between lines so you don't lose your place.
2. Use simple words and avoid unusual words. It's easy to stumble over words you don't usually use.
3. Prepare your notes as though you were telling a story. Use first person, active voice, and contractions to add a natural tone and make delivery easy.

As you move into the extemporaneous style, try these suggestions:

1. Anticipate that you'll be nervous. Good speakers admit to being nervous and claim a little anxiety helps them perform better.
2. As you address the audience, try to make eye contact with only a few people. Select about six scattered widely in the room. Then talk to each of the six one at a time. As you do so, you'll give the impression of speaking to the entire audience. It's easy to talk to one face at a time and often terror to try to look at the entire audience.
3. Don't overdo your gestures. Let them come naturally, but avoid excess hand motion.
4. Insist on a podium for your notes. The podium is also something to hold when your hands might otherwise tremble.
5. Work to avoid *you know*, *OK*, *er*, and other sounds such as throat clearing that will distract from your presentation.
6. Don't use jokes unless you are good at telling them. Jokes are only good when they are used to focus the attention of the audience on a particular topic.
7. Try to develop strong openings and closings. These are the most important part of your talk. The opening gets attention and sets the stage, and the closing summarizes and is the thing your audience will most remember.
9. Dress appropriately and carefully. Appearance and grooming have significant effects on the audience.
10. Try to appear confident and give the impression that you are enjoying yourself.

MAKING AN ORAL REPORT

Oral reports differ from stand-up speeches in several ways. First, the oral report is generally given to an audience familiar to the speaker. The audience and the speaker know quite a bit about each other. Too, the audience will generally be much smaller and the surroundings more intimate for the oral report. In addition, questions are more likely to be asked during the oral report. Obviously, then, the extemporaneous style should be preferred over more formal memorized or written-and-read verbatim presentations.

More often than not, oral reports will be based on formal written reports; they will probably follow the steps in the report process and be organized around a statement of the purpose; a discussion, including research methods and findings; and a summary including the conclusion and implications. Among the reports that can be planned around this outline are reviews of economic conditions; development of new practices or policies; progress reports; personnel, resource, and financial studies; and reports of research.

Visual aids are extremely important tools in oral reports. Just as you incorporate graphics in written reports, you should do so in oral ones. Skilled speakers develop a set of graphics before deciding what they will say about each one. The graphics provide the basis for the presentation. Some guides for using visuals are these:

1. Make the graphic large enough to be seen by the entire audience.
2. Keep the graphic simple. Too much detail may lead the audience to concentrate on unimportant items.
3. Make a separate set of notes for each graphic. As you speak, the audience will look at the graphic more than they will at you. If you are using paperboard displays, you can write light pencil notes on the graphic that will be visible to you but not to the audience.
4. During the presentation, step to one side of the graphic. Use a pointer if necessary, but *always point* to the specific part of the graphic you are talking about—simply nodding your head toward the graphic will not do the job. But also talk to the audience, not to the graphic.

In a presentation to a board of directors, for example, your time allotment will probably be short; and you should stay within the time limits. Therefore, prepare your presentation well in advance and then practice, practice, practice. Your future may depend on this kind of preparation. Although you should attempt to prepare yourself to answer anticipated questions, do not try to make your oral report so thorough that you answer every conceivable question. If you do, you may lose the audience. A sophisticated audience for an oral report may think well ahead of what is being said. Your task will be to get your major points out before someone in the audience makes them for you.

SUMMARY

Listening is our most frequent communication activity; yet, it is one of the most neglected in terms of training. For people preparing to give stand-up speeches or oral presentations to smaller groups, a knowledge of people's bad and good listening habits is helpful. When speakers understand audiences, their ability to communicate is enhanced.

For most oral presentations—speeches or reports—an extemporaneous speaking style is preferred. But we should not confuse extemporaneous speaking with impromptu or "off the cuff" speaking. Extemporaneous speeches are planned and rehearsed to the point where the speaker appears to have a natural style and considerable self confidence. Again, nervousness should not necessarily be associated with lack of self confidence. Good speakers work up anxiety just so they will perform at their peak level.

Oral report presentations concentrate more on content than on speaking style. Yet, speaking style is important. The skillful blending of content, visual displays, and speaking style can build a person's image in the minds of colleagues and superiors. People who are excellent technicians in their own disciplines may never rise to the attention of superiors unless they develop effective speaking abilities.

Examination 1—Chapters 1–4

Fill in the blanks

1. The process of interpreting a message is called __________.
2. The least effective level of communication is the __________ level.
3. Maslow's hierarchy of needs would have most adult Americans at the __________ level.
4. The reaction of the recipient to a message just received is called __________.
5. "Treat adults as adults" is compatible with MacGregor's Theory __________.

True-false

_____ 6. In America, most people are successful in satisfying their self-actualizing needs.

_____ 7. The destination of all human communication is the mind of the receiver.

_____ 8. Theory Y management practices are always superior to Theory X practices.

_____ 9. Two-way communication represents the least effective level of communication.

_____ 10. The two elements contributing to communication effectiveness are availability of feedback and opportunity to observe nonverbal aids.

_____ 11. If a word is commonly used in a reader's business, its use in a letter is acceptable even though it may not be understood by the general population.

_____ 12. Writers should try to avoid using long, complicated words as substitutes for simple words that have the same meanings.

_____ 13. Messages transmitted through words will have greater impact than messages transmitted through action.

_____ 14. The effects of a metacommunication may be either positive or negative.

_____ 15. Kinesic messages are messages picked up "between the lines" of written messages.

_____ 16. A good way to build up a reader's ego is to employ worn expressions.

_____ 17. "Basic fundamentals" is an example of a redundancy.

_____ 18. Compound adjectives are placed *after* nouns instead of *before* them.

_____ 19. Use of strong adjectives and adverbs is associated (in a positive way) with objectivity.

_____ 20. If an idea is to be subordinated, it should be placed in the independent clause of a complex sentence.

_____ 21. Even if a superlative is supported with accompanying data, its use is not recommended.

_____ 22. A good way to emphasize an idea is to place it in the dependent clause of a complex sentence.

_____ 23. Placing a positive idea in one independent clause and a negative idea in an accompanying independent clause is considered a grammatical error.

_____ 24. "Under separate cover" is a good example of a commonly used superlative.

_____ 25. A redundancy is considered a grammatical error.

_____ 26. In a compound sentence, the first clause gets considerably more emphasis than does the second clause.

_____ 27. If an idea would be obvious without expressing it, the idea need not be expressed in words at all.

_____ 28. "I wish I could" illustrates use of the subjunctive mood in stating a negative.

_____ 29. An idea that appears in a short, simple sentence gets more emphasis than does an idea that appears in a complex sentence.

_____ 30. "Exactly identical" is an example of a superlative.

_____ 31. Words joined by a hyphen (or hyphens) and used as one-word modifiers are called "co-ordinate adjectives."

_____ 32. In a passive sentence, the subject is the doer of action.

_____ 33. A word that appears last in a sentence gets more emphasis than does a word that appears in the middle of a sentence.

_____ 34. The purpose of parallel construction is to achieve variety in expression.

_____ 35. "May I have the following information" is considered more diplomatic than "You failed to give sufficient information."

_____ 36. When a sentence contains a series, the units in the series should be expressed in the same way grammatically.

_____ 37. Normally, passive sentences are recommended for conveying pleasant thoughts.

_____ 38. The primary problem that results from a dangling participial phrase is confusion about where action took place.

_____ 39. Normally, a suitable readability level for business people is somewhere between the 8th and the 11th grade levels.

_____ 40. A good transition sentence summarizes a preceding topic and leads a reader to expect the up-coming topic.

_____ 41. Metacommunications that result from grammatical errors are almost sure to be positive.

_____ 42. Some passive sentences reveal the doer of action; others do not.

_____ 43. A refusal stated in the indicative mood is less direct than a refusal stated in the subjunctive mood.

_____ 44. The inductive paragraph arrangement is recommended when persuasion is thought to be necessary.

_____ 45. If a major idea is presented first and then followed by details, the arrangement is said to be deductive.

_____ 46. An "unequivocal" statement is one in which the author tries to escape responsibility for the idea being presented.

_____ 47. In a given piece of writing, all paragraphs should be approximately the same length.

_____ 48. In letters, first and last paragraphs should be longer than paragraphs that appear in the middle.

_____ 49. As sentence subjects, concrete nouns (instead of abstract nouns) are normally preferred.

_____ 50. In sentences that begin with expletives, readers are exposed to the verb before learning what the true subject is.

Now turn to the answers to Examination 1 on page 193. Study the items missed.

Examination 2—Chapters 5–9

Fill in the blanks

1. The outline recommended for refusal letters is

   ____
   ____
   ____
   ____

2. The outline recommended for sales letters is

   ____
   ____
   ____
   ____

True-false

_____ 3. Before composing a letter, a writer should determine the specific purpose of the letter, the points to be included, and the sequence in which to present the points.

_____ 4. Writers need not take time to put an outline on paper; it should merely be kept in mind.

_____ 5. Both routine claim letters and persuasive claim letters should be written deductively.

_____ 6. The words *claim* and *grant* are highly recommended for use in responses to claim letters.

_____ 7. If a request is expected to be granted willingly, the writing should be deductive.

_____ 8. For a letter, to *express* an idea is a more legitimate objective than to *impress* the reader.

_____ 9. As used in the text, "resale" is used to designate a second transaction involving the same product.

_____ 10. Like routine claim letters, letters that ask for credit information are written deductively.

_____ 11. If the anticipated reader reaction is positive, the writing should be inductive.

_____ 12. Putting the pleasant idea in the first sentence has the effect of emphasizing the pleasant idea.

_____ 13. In a letter that conveys a refusal, the reasons for the refusal should be subordinated.

_____ 14. In a letter designed to persuade someone to take action, the action should be mentioned in the first sentence.

_____ 15. A letter that extends credit should say nothing about the basis for doing so.

_____ 16. The primary question in determining whether to write inductively or deductively is "How long is the message?"

_____ 17. The deductive arrangement is recommended for both letters that convey pleasant messages and letters that convey routine messages.

_____ 18. In a letter that conveys a refusal, the refusal should be presented in the last sentence.

_____ 19. A claim letter is a request for an adjustment.

_____ 20. One who writes a routine claim letter assumes the request will be granted quickly and willingly, without persuasion.

_____ 21. Resale and sales-promotional material should not be employed in response to claim letters.

_____ 22. For seeking credit information, form letters are frequently employed.

_____ 23. A letter that contains a refusal should also contain an apology for it.

_____ 24. When circumstances are such that a proposal will probably be rejected unless accompanying explanations are given, the writing should be inductive.

_____ 25. Credit refusals should not employ resale or sales-promotional material.

_____ 26. Reasons that follow a refusal get more attention than do reasons that precede a refusal.

_____ 27. If a deductive refusal conveys the message adequately and promotes the kind of reader-writer relationship desired, the deductive approach is acceptable.

_____ 28. The impatience that may result from an inductive approach to a refusal is more damaging than the anger that may result from a deductive approach to a refusal.

_____ 29. A good closing sentence for a refusal letter is "Thank you for your interest."

_____ 30. "If you have further questions, please don't hesitate to write" is a good closing sentence for most refusal letters.

_____ 31. "We trust this explanation is satisfactory" is a good sentence for closing a refusal letter.

_____ 32. Credit refusals should reveal a willingness to reconsider when new information is presented.

_____ 33. Before persuasive letters ask for action, they should reveal advantages of taking action.

_____ 34. In a persuasive claim letter, the action desired should be stated in the first sentence.

_____ 35. Just as a report should have a theme, so should a sales letter have a central idea that permeates the entire letter.

_____ 36. The specific action wanted is *discussed* in the last paragraph of a sales letter, but the desired action should be *determined* before the first paragraph is written.

_____ 37. Compared with most other letters, sales letters are longer.

_____ 38. In persuasive letters, specific language is normally less effective than general language.

_____ 39. Product-centered writing is more effective than reader-centered writing.

_____ 40. Most of the space in a sales letter should be devoted to the presentation of evidence.

_____ 41. Good collection methods are based on assumptions that the debtor doesn't know he or she owes but, at the same time, doesn't mind being asked to pay.

_____ 42. An inquiry letter is prepared on the assumption that the debtor has a problem that makes payment difficult.

_____ 43. Compared with most persuasive letters, collection letters are shorter.

_____ 44. At the appeals stage, a collection letter should include three or more appeals.

_____ 45. The traditional three Cs of credit are character, capacity, and conditions.

_____ 46. Telegrams should be reserved for late stages in the collection process.

_____ 47. An assumption underlying all credit transactions is that the lender can trust the debtor.

_____ 48. In a collection series, an appeal to fair play is effective at the ultimatum stage.

_____ 49. Form letters should always be prepared in such a way that the recipient has difficulty identifying them as forms.

_____ 50. Debtors may be classified according to their past practices of paying.

_____ 51. Compared with persuasive letters, letters of condolence are relatively short.

_____ 52. Condolences by telegram are considered to be in bad taste.

_____ 53. Handwriting is considered inappropriate for congratulatory letters.

_____ 54. Both letters of condolence and congratulation should be acknowledged.

_____ 55. If negatives are included in a recommendation letter, they should normally be subordinated.

_____ 56. Letters of introduction should be sent only to close acquaintances.

_____ 57. In a letter of invitation, the inside address is placed *after* the letter.

_____ 58. If an invitation includes an RSVP, the invitation should be acknowledged promptly.

_____ 59. Normally, resignations are expected to be in written form.

_____ 60. One whose resignation has been encouraged should (in the letter of resignation) resist any temptation to take a "parting shot" at the employer.

Now turn to the answers to Examination 2 on page 193. Study the items missed.

Examination 3—Chapters 10–14

Write your answers, either true (T) or false (F); *a, b, c,* or *d;* or the necessary words on the appropriate lines.

_____ 1. Ordinarily, the closing paragraph of an application letter invites the reader to send a letter that reveals whether the applicant has been selected.

_____ 2. Before preparing a résumé, job seekers should make a written list of facts about the job and another list of facts about themselves.

_____ 3. In an application letter, good writing can be counted on to compensate for poor training.

_____ 4. Employers normally prefer that the application letter and résumé be combined into a single page.

_____ 5. An applicant should prepare a résumé *after* having written the letter of application.

_____ 6. The résumé should repeat the information presented in the letter of application.

_____ 7. Normally, the résumé is referred to in the first or second paragraphs of the application letter.

_____ 8. On a résumé, phrases (instead of complete sentences) are preferred.

_____ 9. When the points that deserve emphasis are considered, "personal data" will be presented in some position other than in the first section of a résumé.

_____ 10. A college graduate who is short on experience and long on education should let "Experience" appear as the first section of a résumé.

_____ 11. An applicant whose experience has been in an assembly line should omit that experience from a résumé designed to get an office job.

_____ 12. An applicant who has a wide variety of experiences should present them in chronological order on the data sheet.

_____ 13. Applicants with a wide variety of experience are strongly encouraged to list all of them on the résumé.

_____ 14. On the résumé, listing only the most pertinent courses is better than listing all courses taken.

_____ 15. Applicants are encouraged to limit the résumé to one page because doing so forces them to include only the most pertinent information.

_____ 16. Specifics about duties performed should be omitted from résumés.

_____ 17. Application letters employ the general sequence of ideas recommended for sales letters.

_____ 18. An application letter should begin with "I should like to apply for . . ."

_____ 19. Normally, application letters should be shorter than most other letters—no more than half a page.

_____ 20. "May I have an interview at your convenience" is recommended as a desirable sentence for the last paragraph of an application letter.

_____ 21. Just as a sales letter alludes to the central selling point in the last paragraph, so should an application letter allude to the primary qualification in the last paragraph.

_____ 22. Preferably, an unsolicited application letter should include a paragraph of discussion about salary.

_____ 23. In solicited and unsolicited application letters, the first paragraphs are very similar.

24. The real basis for a report is its contribution to __________ solving or __________ making.

_____ 25. Null hypotheses state problems in such a way that bias is apparently eliminated.

_____ 26. Library materials are described as secondary sources.

_____ 27. Good questionnaire development calls for the most difficult items to be placed first.

28. The U.S. Census is a form of __________ __________ research.

29. When only a portion of total population is surveyed, but findings are attributed to the entire population, the portion surveyed is called a ____________________.

30. Research involving applying a variable to one of two identical samples and measuring the resulting difference is called __________ research.

31. The briefest thing you can record and still assist in recall is a ______________ ______________.

_____ 32. The report process involves constantly condensing large amounts of information.

_____ 33. Using criteria as divisions of the findings section makes comparison more effective.

34. In most reports the two most important of the four problem-solving steps are __________ and __________, while the __________ and __________ are of secondary interest from the reader's point of view.

_____ 35. A feature of the decimal system of outlining is that it is expandable.

_____ 36. A major principle in outline preparation is that any part must be divided into at least two parts or it should not be divided.

_____ 37. When a report is organized with all the parts preceding the conclusion, the organization is said to be

a. Inductive
b. Deductive
c. Normal

_____ 38. The four-step method of problem solving is an inductive method.

_____ 39. Contents pages should include all headings used in the body of the report.

40. When a separate summary page is not included, the summary may be incorporated in the ____________________.

____ 41. Reports may grow in formality simply because of size.

____ 42. Addenda items contain evidence that lends credibility to the report.

____ 43. Tables contain easily understandable material and, therefore, do not require interpretation by the writer.

____ 44. A graphic presentation should be placed at the end of a report so it will not interrupt the written portion.

45. __________ charts are desirable to give impact to the distribution of parts of a whole.

46. To compare quantities, the __________ chart is perhaps the most effective presentation.

47. Changes in quantitative data over time are best depicted in __________charts.

____ 48. When negative amounts are to be shown in a line chart, the quantitative scale may be started at less than zero.

____ 49. Text sentences introducing graphics should always begin with "As shown in Figure. . . ."

____ 50. In most graphics, the horizontal axis should represent amounts.

Now turn to the answers to Examination 3 on page 194. Study the items missed.

Examination 4—Chapters 15–18

Write your answers—true (T) or false (F); *a, b, c,* or *d;* or the necessary words on the appropriate lines.

_____ 1. Personal pronouns should be avoided in all report writing.

_____ 2. In passive construction, the subject of the sentence is the receiver of the action.

_____ 3. Common language usage in reports enables the writer to simplify the interpretation of large figures.

_____ 4. Which of the following is not part of a definition?

a. Term
b. Family
c. Class
d. Differentiation

_____ 5. "Customers Want Increased Services" is an example of a talking heading.

_____ 6. Tying parts of a report together is accomplished through tabulation techniques.

_____ 7. A judgment is the writer's opinion of the good or bad of something.

_____ 8. An inference is a statement about the unknown based on the known.

_____ 9. Weasel words should be avoided.

_____ 10. Documentation is an unnecessary burden, because its only purpose is to add authority to reports.

_____ 11. Terminal footnoting is an efficient method, because it combines footnotes and bibliography.

_____ 12. Although headings should be used in reports, the report should be understandable without the help of headings.

_____ 13. Although memorandums are reports, they may be psychologically organized as are letters.

_____ 14. Memorandums, unlike other reports, may rely on the subject line for thought.

15. A good method to use in reviewing the draft of a report is to read it __________.

_____ 16. The distinction between informal reports and formal ones is clear cut.

_____ 17. Textual introductions to tables or graphs need only call attention to the figure; in this way, the reader can do his or her own interpreting of the material.

_____ 18. Emotional terms should be avoided in reports.

_____ 19. Repetition of a word or an idea is a poor way to develop transition.

_____ 20. Talking about large amounts of quantitative data in terms of percentages is using common language.

_____ 21. The author's given name appears first in a footnote.

_____ 22. Documentation can be made by using incidental reference to sources such as "According to the Bureau of Agriculture. . . ."

_____ 23. Reports can't analyze, people can.

_____ 24. The introductory headings in a report may be eliminated because people expect the introduction to be at the beginning of a report.

_____ 25. Conclusions in a report may be described as generalizations about the findings.

_____ 26. Recommendations in a report should not be based on the conclusions.

_____ 27. The best time to edit your report is during your writing of the rough draft.

_____ 28. Most reports flow upward in the organization.

_____ 29. Memorandums only flow downward in the organization.

_____ 30. Memorandums play only a minor role in an organization's internal written communication.

_____ 31. The printed headings on memorandum forms save typing time; otherwise, they are of little value.

_____ 32. The distinction between a long memorandum and a short report is clear cut.

_____ 33. The use of informal language in a memorandum is a distinguishing difference between the memorandum and a formal research report.

_____ 34. All memorandums should be organized deductively.

_____ 35. Our most frequently used communication skill is speaking.

_____ 36. It is impossible for people to over-listen.

_____ 37. When people think they have problems, it is a good idea to give them advice but not to waste time listening to them get things off their chests.

_____ 38. Across the office desk is a good place for a serious discussion.

_____ 39. Which of the following terms does not belong?

a. *Impromptu*
b. *Persuasive*
c. *Memorized*
d. *Extemporaneous*

_____ 40. Memorizing as a speech method probably has the fewest limitations of any style.

41. For technical, complex subject matter, the speech style most appropriate is __________-__________-__________.

42. Professional speakers most often use the __________ speaking style.

_____ 43. Nervousness is a sign of lack of experience.

_____ 44. Using a few unusual words is a good practice in speaking because it will keep the audience awake.

_____ 45. Oral reporting differs from public speaking in the familiarity of the speaker and the audience.

_____ 46. Visual aids can form the basis for the oral presentation.

_____ 47. Public speeches are generally longer than oral reports.

_____ 48. A good oral report makes use of as many jokes and stories as possible to support the points made.

_____ 49. Questions from the audience are more likely to be raised during a public speech than during an oral report.

_____ 50. Written-and-read style is most appropriate for oral reporting.

Now turn to the answers to Examination 4 on page 195. Study the items missed.

Answers to Examinations

Answers to Examination 1, Chapters 1–4

1. decoding
2. 3d
3. social or ego
4. feedback
5. Y
6. F
7. T
8. F
9. F
10. T
11. T
12. T
13. F
14. T
15. F
16. F
17. T
18. F
19. F
20. F
21. F
22. F
23. F
24. F
25. T
26. F
27. T
28. T
29. T
30. F
31. F
32. F
33. F
34. F
35. T
36. T
37. T
38. F
39. T
40. T
41. F
42. T
43. F
44. T
45. T
46. F
47. F
48. F
49. T
50. T

Answers to Examination 2, Chapters 5–9

1. Neutral statement that leads to reasons
   Facts, analysis, reasons
   Unpleasant message
   Related idea that takes emphasis away from the unpleasant
2. Get attention
   Introduce proposal (product)
   Provide evidence
   Encourage action
3. T
4. F

5. F
6. F
7. T
8. T
9. F
10. T
11. F
12. T
13. F
14. F
15. F
16. F
17. T
18. F
19. T
20. T
21. F
22. T
23. F
24. T
25. F
26. F
27. T
28. F
29. F
30. F
31. F
32. T
33. T
34. F
35. T
36. T
37. T
38. F
39. F
40. T
41. F
42. T
43. T
44. F
45. F
46. T
47. T
48. F
49. F
50. T
51. T
52. F
53. F
54. T
55. T
56. T
57. T
58. T
59. T
60. T

Answers to Examination 3, Chapters 10–14

1. F
2. T
3. F
4. F
5. F
6. F
7. F
8. T
9. T
10. F
11. F
12. F
13. F
14. T
15. T
16. F
17. T
18. F
19. F
20. F
21. T
22. F
23. F
24. problem, decision
25. T
26. T
27. F
28. normative survey

29. sample
30. experimental
31. cue note
32. T
33. T
34. findings and conclusions, purpose and methods
35. T
36. T
37. *a*
38. T
39. T
40. letter of transmittal
41. T
42. T
43. F
44. F
45. pie
46. bar
47. line
48. F
49. F
50. F

Answers to Examination 4, Chapters 15–18

1. F
2. T
3. T
4. *c*
5. T
6. F
7. T
8. T
9. F
10. F
11. T
12. T
13. T
14. F
15. aloud
16. F
17. F
18. T
19. F
20. T
21. T
22. T
23. T
24. T
25. T
26. F
27. F
28. T
29. F
30. F
31. F
32. F
33. T
34. F
35. F
36. F
37. F
38. F
39. *b*
40. F
41. written-and-read
42. extemporaneous
43. F
44. F
45. T
46. T
47. T
48. F
49. F
50. F

Glossary/Index

T

U–W